To Samye, who gives me purpose every day.

MEANT FOR MORE

WAKING UP TO THE LIFE YOU WERE SENT TO LIVE

MEANT FOR MORE

WAKING UP TO THE LIFE YOU WERE SENT TO LIVE

DUSTIN PETERSON

CFI
An imprint of Cedar Fort, Inc.
Springville, Utah

Paperback ISBN 13: 978-1-4621-5043-4
eBook ISBN 13: 978-1-4621-5044-1

Published by CFI, an imprint of Cedar Fort, Inc.
2373 W. 700 S., Suite 100, Springville, UT 84663
Distributed by Cedar Fort, Inc., www.cedarfort.com

Library of Congress Cataloging Number: 2025947330

Cover design by Mario Padilla and Shawnda T. Craig

Edited and Typeset by Liz Kazandzhy

Printed in the United States of America

10 9 8 7 6 5 4 3 2 1

Printed on acid-free paper

Contents

Acknowledgments

Publishing this project became its own test of purpose. I began writing it seven years ago, driven by a desire to help others maximize their divine potential. But like many of you, I soon met the "villains of purpose" outlined in chapter 5—resistance, doubt, distraction. Hence the seven-year journey.

Thankfully, I didn't walk that path alone. God placed people along the way who challenged my assumptions, stretched my thinking, and reminded me to keep going.

First and always, to Samye—my eternal companion and steady rock. Nothing I've written or accomplished would exist without your unwavering support and quiet strength. You embody what it means to live on purpose. As my mom always says, "There's only *one* Samye in the world." She's right.

To our four incredible children—Halle, Bennett, Miles, and Rowe—thank you for being my favorite classroom. You've taught me more about purpose, joy, and resilience than any textbook or mentor ever could.

To our extended family—parents, in-laws, and loved ones—thank you for cheering me on, buying the first copies, and always believing the best about my work. Your encouragement is felt and deeply appreciated.

To the clients, leaders, and friends who've welcomed me into your journeys—thank you for trusting me with your stories. You've shown me that purpose is not theory; it's real life. A special thanks to Keith Warner, Bryce Wong, and Ryan Addams for allowing me to share parts of your story in these pages.

To the Church leaders, mentors, and teachers who've shaped my spiritual foundation—thank you for showing me what it looks like to lead with both conviction and compassion. You've been living examples of what I've tried to put into words.

To the team at Cedar Fort—thank you for going another round with me after *Talented*. Your belief in this message has brought it to life.

And finally, to the reader holding this book: Thank you for daring to explore your purpose. May this be a catalyst—not an endpoint—and may you walk forward with courage, clarity, and trust in the One who sent you.

Introduction: The Search for Meaning

"What should I do with my life?" I call it the universal question because it's the one question every person eventually asks. It's closely related to "Why am I here?" and "What's my purpose?" Whether it surfaces during a quiet walk, a late-night worry session, a personal loss, or a major life decision, the search for meaning is universal. We long to know that our lives are part of a bigger story—that we aren't just wandering through random events but are part of a divine plan. We wonder if we have a unique, specific, and individual purpose, something meant just for us.

As members of The Church of Jesus Christ of Latter-day Saints, we hold a profound belief: Our lives have eternal significance. Our existence isn't a cosmic accident; it was designed with intention and purpose. But acknowledging that truth is only the beginning. The harder question follows: How do we discover our specific purpose? How do we uncover the individual mission God crafted for us before the world began?

This book is about that very search. It's about discovering why you're here on earth, placed in your specific family, community, time, and circumstances. It's about aligning your life with God's will so you can fulfill the work He uniquely prepared for you.

According to Barna Group's "State of Calling" study (2018), most adults say they believe they have a calling—but only a small percentage feel confident they're actually living it out.[1] That gap creates what Barna calls a spiritual identity crisis. People want their lives to matter, but they don't know how to move from belief to action. That's exactly what this book is designed to help with.

Elder Alan T. Phillips reminds us, "Where there is design, there is a designer. Your life has meaning and purpose."[2] Our Father in Heaven, the great Designer, imbued your life with a personal and sacred purpose. Through a combination of personal experiences, modern prophetic teachings, and practical tools, this book will guide you toward discovering that purpose.

Think of it! Your life has a specific, individualized, personal, meaningful purpose waiting to be clarified. Imagine the energy you'd feel waking up every day to that clear purpose, aligning your actions to a specific intent. Many years ago, I clarified my purpose, and that clarity has made all the difference. My goal is to walk you through the same shift in mindset and process I used to gain this clarity.

Rather than spending chapters philosophizing about purpose, let's jump into how you can actively find it—starting right now.

1

What Is Purpose and Why Does It Matter?

"He who has a why to live can bear almost any how."
—Friedrich Nietzsche[3]

Purpose.

It's a word tossed around in conversations, self-help books, and leadership seminars—often attached to promises of a more fulfilling life. But for all its popularity, purpose remains a deeply misunderstood and sometimes intimidating concept.

For many of us, it feels elusive.

Am I supposed to know it already? Did I miss my chance? What if I never figure it out?

We fear that if we don't discover our purpose quickly enough, we'll somehow live an inferior life—one that's less impactful, less joyful, and less aligned with God's design for us.

But here's the truth:

Your life has a purpose. It had a purpose before you were born.

It will have a purpose long after today's anxieties fade into memory.

As members of The Church of Jesus Christ of Latter-day Saints, we believe that our existence is no accident. Before we ever set foot on earth, we lived with heavenly parents who prepared us for this mortal journey. We were taught. We were loved. And we were given assignments—missions so specific and individual that no one else could fulfill them quite the way we could.

Elder Bruce R. McConkie of the Quorum of the Twelve Apostles said this:

> All the spirits of men, while yet in the Eternal Presence, developed aptitudes, talents, capacities, and abilities of every sort, kind, and degree. During the long expanse of life which then was, an infinite variety of talents and abilities came into being. As the ages rolled, no two spirits remained alike. Mozart became a musician; Einstein centered his interest in mathematics; Michelangelo turned his attention to painting. . . . Abraham and Moses and all of the prophets sought and obtained the talent for spirituality. . . .
>
> When we pass from preexistence to mortality, we bring with us the traits and talents there developed. True, we forget what went before because we are here being tested, but the capacities and abilities that then were ours are yet resident within us. Mozart is still a musician; Einstein retains his mathematical abilities; Michelangelo his artistic talent; Abraham, Moses, and the prophets their spiritual talents and abilities. . . . And all men with their infinitely varied talents and personalities pick up the course of progression where they left it off when they left the heavenly realms.[4]

We didn't just frolic around in the premortal realm, enjoying the beauties of that splendid world. This was a time of active development and of becoming more like our Father. We eventually hit a ceiling, a point after which progression would be limited if we couldn't have a mortal experience with a physical body. The plan was put forth, and Adam and Eve started their journey, opening the way for the rest of us to take the next step.

You were born into existence on this earth and brought with you a divine purpose that began in the premortal life.

Purpose isn't just about career choices.

It isn't limited to a job title, a calling, or a set of hobbies.

Your purpose is your reason for being.

It's the guiding force that shapes how you spend your time, how you face your trials, and how you leave your mark on the world.

And most importantly, purpose is powerful.

There's a longing for clarity, meaning, and direction—not just to make it through the day but to live for something that actually matters. In fact, purpose isn't just a spiritual longing—it's a human developmental need.

A Closer Look: What Stanford Research Says About Purpose

In a culture obsessed with personal success, self-expression, and chasing "what feels good," the concept of purpose can feel both overused and underdefined. But for Dr. Bill Damon, a developmental psychologist at Stanford University and founding director of the Stanford Center on Adolescence, purpose isn't just a nice idea. It's a critical piece of human development—and one most people are missing.

Damon defines purpose as "a stable and generalized intention to accomplish something that is at once meaningful to the self and of consequence to the world beyond the self."[5] In other words, purpose isn't just about what you love. It's about what you're willing to contribute. What you're committed to. What you're building that matters to someone other than you.

In his groundbreaking book *The Path to Purpose*, Damon studied hundreds of young people across backgrounds, interests, and belief systems to understand how purpose emerges—and what happens when it doesn't. The results were sobering.

He found that *only about 20 percent of youth* in his sample could articulate anything close to a purpose in life. The rest fell into three categories:

- **The Disengaged**, who weren't searching for purpose at all;
- **The Dabblers**, who had interests but no focus or sense of direction; and
- **The Dreamers**, who had lofty goals but no concrete action or connection to service.

What's fascinating is that Damon's findings didn't just apply to young adults. As he expanded his work, he saw the same patterns repeated in adults across life stages. Many people—even high-functioning, busy, successful people—were simply going through the motions. Their calendars were full, but their lives were not anchored by any sense of deep meaning or calling.

This "purpose deficit," Damon argues, has serious consequences. Individuals without a sense of purpose are more likely to experience anxiety, disengagement, addiction, and aimlessness. They may succeed by outward standards, but inwardly, they feel restless or stuck.

That same fog follows many of us into adulthood. We keep ourselves busy, but deep down we wonder: Is any of this adding up to something that matters?

The good news is that purpose isn't something you either have or don't. It's something that can be *discovered* and *developed.* In fact, Damon found that people who did live with purpose often found it through reflection—by making sense of past experiences, pain, passions, and moments of service. The best predictors of purpose weren't raw talent or even passion—they were intentional reflection and meaningful connection. Said a different way, your purpose isn't what you do (as in your daily work or the manifestations or expressions of your efforts) but rather why you do it and the motivating forces that drive you.

But that's exactly why your story matters. When you slow down and trace where God has been moving—even in the shadows—you start to see that the ingredients for purpose are already there. They just need to be named, claimed, and aligned with something bigger than you.

Because the truth is, you don't have to drift. You don't have to settle. And you're never too late to live on purpose. You didn't step out of line in the premortal existence and miss your chance at being assigned a life purpose.

In my work, coaching leaders at organizations and career-counseling individuals through life transitions, I'm always amazed at the number of people who feel they are devoid of purpose and just floating. They tend to believe that everyone around them has it figured out and that they're the one person on earth who missed their calling. Yet as I often tell them, which of us was armed with a clear and intentional plan at a young age for identifying our life's work? Who among us was taught in grade school how to clarify a meaningful goal toward which to direct our lives?

I certainly wasn't. I drifted through school, more interested in how to survive each class and advance through each grade. My existential reflections consisted of wondering why the Dallas sports teams of my youth seemed to languish more than other cities and why it was that we didn't eat more bacon as a society, delicious as it is.

And yet I eventually came to understand my purpose in my twenties and began to fully embrace it in my thirties. Some of the people I coach find theirs earlier, but for many, it happens later—in their forties, fifties, or even beyond. The good news is that *when* you discover your purpose matters less than how you choose to magnify it once you do.

So how do you figure it out? How do you know what your individual purpose is?

This can seem so ambiguous. "I want to be a good dad" or "I want to provide for my family" can feel important but too general. The application of it can seem so daunting or unclear.

Nine times out of ten, when I ask people "What's your purpose?" the answer is "I just want to help people." Right. You and the gas station attendant and the grocery worker and the server at Chick-fil-A. But there has to be something more specific to you, right?

I believe this is a great purpose in life—to discover your purpose and to give your whole heart and soul to it.

I also believe you have a very specific purpose, one that you are uniquely prepared to accomplish through your special combination of personality, talents, aptitudes, ambitions, relationships, and set of life circumstances.

First, let's define "purpose" more clearly to know what we're aiming for.

What Is Purpose?

Bill Damon gave some clues above—purpose is stable, intentional, meaningful to self, and serves a greater good. I also love the definition of purpose from Angela Duckworth, author of *Grit: The Power of Passion and Perseverance*, which echoes similar sentiments. She says, "Your purpose is your intention to contribute to the well-being of other people. It is a tremendously powerful source of motivation."[6]

I love this for a few reasons:

- It's intentional, as in "on purpose" (pun intended). It's something we set out to do specifically. It's not passive or accidental, and it doesn't happen *to us.* We happen *to it.*
- It's other-focused. If my purpose is only focused on me, it doesn't have pulling power. I was working with a client many years ago, trying to help him boil down his purpose to a statement of power. He said, "I think I exist to amass knowledge." I said, "Oh, I like that, but to what end? Like, why do you want to become all-knowing?" I pushed him on it. He thought about it and said, "I guess I want to learn everything so I can lift other people." The moment he said that, you could feel the energy shift in the conversation. It had pulling power. It was no longer about him and his goals but rather about lifting others to a higher plane. It's not about you. Purpose is other-focused. In fact, I often teach that the difference between purpose and goals is that purpose is about others, whereas goals are often (not always, but often) self-serving. "I want to lose ten pounds" is usually about you. Or "I want to save a million dollars" is about your future. But purpose is bigger than you.
- It's a contribution. Your purpose is about adding value and bringing the best of what you do well to bear. A few years ago, I published my book *Talented* about how to discover your God-given talents. An interesting thing occurred. People would read the book, discover their gifts, and then call me to ask, "Now what?" I was always a bit perplexed. Go use them! Put them to work! Serve others! One day, I realized what people were really asking, which was "Where do I aim them?" In other words, what's my purpose to point my talents at? This makes sense to me. Talents are what you do best, and purpose is where to direct them.

- It's motivating. This is key. Purpose is a powerful source of motivation! It drives you. It pulls you forward. When I think of my purpose, it gets me up and moving. I've had times and seasons in my life where I lose my sense of purpose, and the result is a palpable feeling of discouragement and stuckness. I'll spiral and feel lost, and then, usually in a moment of despair, I'll recall why I exist and my specific purpose on earth. Then I'll instantly feel that rapid heartbeat and warmth in my body that drives me forward to do what I do best for the benefit of others.

In fact, purpose has been associated with some pretty incredible outcomes. People who know their purpose . . .

- Quadruple the likelihood of being engaged at work[7]
- Live up to seven years longer[8]
- Experience a 42 percent increase in happiness[9]
- Have better quality sleep[10]
- Have improved impulse control[11]
- Are able to stave off depression[12]
- Reduce their mortality rate by 23 percent[13]

I even read a study a number of years ago from AARP that people who have a clearly articulated purpose statement are 125 percent more likely to get a flu shot. Ha!

Why would that be? Why is purpose associated with such great outcomes? Perhaps because when I know my "why" and am in pursuit of something greater, I'm less likely to disengage at work, rest easier at night, control my impulses (such as limiting the number of nights that I attack a bowl of Fruity Pebbles before bed), and therefore live longer.

Not only this, but one study from researchers published in *Leadership Quarterly* found that people who discover their purpose are more resilient in the face of setbacks, experience higher job satisfaction, are more productive, and experience "flow" more often, which is the sense of getting lost in your work so that time seems to fly by.[14]

Purpose makes you happier at work and better at what you do. And happiness plus productivity generally equates to greater success, resulting in not only intrinsic satisfaction but extrinsic rewards, like being paid, promoted, and rewarded for doing what you love!

Likewise, Anthony Burrow, who leads the Purpose and Identity Processes Lab at Cornell University, defines purpose as a central, self-organizing life aim that guides behavior and provides a sense of meaning.[15] His studies reveal that individuals with a strong sense of purpose experience greater psychological resilience, improved health outcomes, and enhanced cognitive functioning.

One of Burrow's notable findings is the relationship between purpose and stress. He discovered that individuals who possess a clear sense of purpose are better equipped to handle stress and recover from adverse events. This resilience stems from the motivational framework that purpose provides, enabling individuals to navigate challenges with a sense of direction and meaning.

Moreover, Burrow's research indicates that purpose contributes to better mental health by reducing symptoms of depression and anxiety. Individuals with a defined purpose are more likely to engage in health-promoting behaviors and maintain social connections, both of which are crucial for mental well-being. If your purpose is clear, you eat right, exercise, and get enough sleep!

In practical terms, Burrow suggests that cultivating purpose doesn't necessarily require grand achievements. Instead, it involves engaging in activities that align with one's values and contribute to something beyond the self. This could be as simple as mentoring others, participating in community service, or pursuing personal growth endeavors.

It's clear that our understanding of purpose is not merely a lofty ideal but a tangible asset that enhances our daily lives. By identifying and committing to meaningful goals, we can foster resilience, improve our mental health, and lead more fulfilling lives.

Purpose Is Powerful

Suffice it to say, purpose is powerful. The good news of the gospel of Jesus Christ is that life has a purpose! And the even greater news is that you have a specific purpose, one unique to you.

Elder John C. Pingree Jr. taught the following:

> God has important work for each of us. Speaking to sisters but teaching truths that apply to all, President Spencer W. Kimball taught: "Before we came [to earth, we] were given certain assignments. . . . While we do not now remember the particulars, this does not alter the glorious reality of what we once agreed to." What an ennobling truth! Our Heavenly Father has specific and significant things for you and me to accomplish (see Ephesians 2:10).
>
> These divine assignments are not reserved for a privileged few but are for all of us—regardless of gender, age, race, nationality, income level, social status, or Church calling. Every one of us has a meaningful role to play in furthering God's work (see Moses 1:39).[16]

In the premortal realm, you were given specific assignments. President Nelson said, "The Lord has more in mind for you than you have in mind for yourself! You have been reserved and preserved for this time and place. The Lord needs you to change the world. As you accept and follow His will for you, you will find yourself accomplishing the impossible!"[17]

Purpose as an Anchor

It might sound lofty to talk about "divine missions" and "eternal impact," but purpose also plays an intensely practical role in your everyday life.

Purpose anchors you when life gets turbulent. For example, if you lose your job or a diagnosis shakes your world, it's easy to feel untethered—like everything solid beneath you just gave way. But if you've named your purpose, it gives you something stable to hold on to. You may not control the storm, but you remember why you're still standing. Purpose becomes your anchor, reminding you who you are and what matters most, even when everything else feels uncertain.

Purpose motivates you when circumstances seem overwhelming. When your schedule is maxed out, your energy is depleted, and the pressure feels unbearable, purpose can give you a reason to keep going. You don't move forward because it's easy—you move forward because you know you're called. When the "why" is clear, you find the strength to face the "how." Purpose lifts your eyes from the mess and fixes them on the mission.

Purpose lifts you when disappointment threatens to drown your spirit. Let's say you pour yourself into something—a relationship, a project, a dream—and it doesn't work out the way you hoped. The door closes. The silence lingers. That's when purpose steps in. It whispers, "This isn't the end." Even when the outcome falls short, purpose reminds you that your obedience still mattered, your effort still counted, and your story isn't over yet.

A number of times in my career, I've put myself out there or applied for new opportunities that haven't panned out. I can think of a moment in particular when I was sitting on the couch watching general conference and felt inspired that I needed to apply for a certain university role. I wasn't even sure the role was posted or existed, but a quick search on the university website showed that the role had just been created and was in active recruitment. I took it as a sign. It was such a random and striking thought that I figured I'd better take action.

Over the following weeks, I cleaned up my CV, requested letters of recommendation from mentors and peers, collected old teaching evaluations from my time at Rice University and the University of Nevada, Las Vegas, and put forward my best application package. I tried to push the role out of my mind and let the process take its course.

After several weeks of waiting, I was notified that my application was declined and that I wasn't even being considered for first-round interviews. Like, I didn't even get the robo-interview where they make sure you're human and not some bot applying from a foreign country! I was so discouraged and confused. Was I inspired? Where did that thought come from? Why did I go through that process?

I reflected and processed this experience for some time but ultimately landed on this one key thought: The outcome of this process in no way changes my ability to maximize my individual purpose here on earth. My purpose is not bound by opportunities that others give me, nor is it at the mercy of someone else's approval. My purpose is mine to manifest, and this one rejection doesn't impede my ability to make it happen right where I am.

Purpose is an anchor.

Pause for a second and really let that sink in.

Living with purpose doesn't just help you feel better about life. It actually helps you live better—longer, stronger, and more joyfully.

But more than that, purpose connects us to the eternal plan of happiness that our Heavenly Father designed for us.

Purpose is woven into the very fabric of the plan of salvation.

- You lived with God before you came to earth (see Jeremiah 1:5).
- You agreed to come here, trusting in the Savior's Atonement to redeem you.
- You were prepared for specific missions.
- You are being shaped, right now, by mortal experiences designed to refine you into the person God knows you can become.

In other words, you are here on purpose—for a purpose.

When You Don't Know Your Purpose

Let me be honest: There are seasons when your purpose feels murky.

I remember one such season vividly.

When I began my career, I felt totally stuck. I was at a crossroads and losing energy fast. The previous year had been glorious—I had married the woman of my dreams, moved to a new home (a.k.a. a crusty apartment in downtown Dallas), and started a new job. I was bright-eyed and ready to fulfill my mission on earth. Then reality hit.

At work, I had been assigned to work on the healthcare and hospitality team of a large public relations agency. Specifically, one of my jobs was to sit in a call booth and cold-call major media publications to pitch them on writing about my client. Unfortunately, my client was GlaxoSmithKline, and more specifically (and even more unfortunately), Beano.

Beano is a natural enzyme that fights gas. Yep, my job was to call editors and pitch them on the virtues of putting an extra-strength gas-fighting enzyme on the cover of the magazine. Suffice it to say, it was a disaster. Day after day, I sat in that little phone booth getting rejected, hung up on, and demoralized.

I remember staring at the blank wall in front of me, getting up the courage to pick up the phone and get shamed by another busy editor in chief, and wondering, "What am I doing with my life?" Like, is this what God has in store for me? This is the promise of my future? The Beano guy?

One day, I came home from work and broke down to my wife. She was standing in the kitchen, eight months pregnant, and cooking noodles in a boiling pot of water. I leaned against the living room wall to debrief the day, and she could sense something was wrong. As we talked, I slid lower and lower, then slumped down the wall into a semi-fetal position.

Imagine it: a 6'5" man coming home to an unsuspecting pregnant wife and curling up on the floor. She looked at me and asked what was wrong.

"I can't do it anymore," I said, exasperated. "I hate my job."

She looked at me perplexed but patiently asked, "Okay. What do you want to do instead?"

"I don't know," I muttered. "That's the problem."

She asked what I wished I could do more of. Again, I didn't know. Frustrated, I said, "I just don't feel like I'm helping anyone. I'm spinning my wheels and getting nowhere."

She picked up on the scent and pursued it. "How do you want to help people?" she asked.

"I don't know," I said. "I just want to help people grow. Help them tap their potential. I want to help them *maximize* their potential."

The flame of energy started to flicker and brighten.

"What would that look like?" she asked.

I didn't know, and it would take some time to sort it out, but that singular statement—*to maximize human potential*—became my rallying cry, my purpose. All other decisions about my career were filtered through that statement. Does it help me maximize others' potential? Then I'll do it.

That little flame of desire—shaky and tentative at first—became the fire that fueled the next decade of my life. From graduate school at Indiana University to jobs in leadership development and now to leading Proof Leadership Group, my desire to help others maximize their potential has driven each move and clarified each step. The outcomes have been powerful. I can honestly say that I've experienced many of the results previously cited in research around purpose: less stress, more engagement, higher energy, more prosperity, less likelihood to eat a nightly bowl of Fruity Pebbles, *and* I got a flu shot. Purpose facilitates decision-making.

Perhaps your purpose has become murky. Maybe you're wandering a bit in the desert. You might even feel like you're stuck on "repeat," acting out the same day over and over. If so, I get it. Also, you're normal. This doesn't mean you're the one person who is devoid of purpose—it just might mean that you need to get some clarity. You may have drifted, or your daily actions may not align with your overarching purpose.

Again, our sense of meaning and purpose can ebb and flow. Two things I've found consistently among the leaders I work with as a trainer and executive coach are that people seem to either have (1) a clearly defined purpose without day-to-day activities to match, or (2) they have lots of meaningful daily actions but no clearly defined purpose to drive toward. In either case, the result is the same.

Flatness. Stuckness. And a general sense of malaise.

Imagine my surprise in 2020, after a strong fifteen-year career in leadership development and career coaching, when I hit a wall. I had emerged from my Beano funk, found a new line of work, pursued education, joined amazing companies, and ultimately built a successful business. But there I was, forty years old and feeling stuck again. The reasons merit a book of their own, but the SparkNotes version is simple: I was doing lots of things each day—important things—but had drifted from my ultimate purpose, to *maximize human potential.*

A clear purpose helps you self-assess, realign, and move forward. But again, purpose is about more than career clarity.

The Gospel Power Behind Purpose

As we've covered so far, purpose isn't just a "nice to have."

It's a spiritual necessity.

In Moses 1:39, the Lord declares, "For behold, this is my work and my glory—to bring to pass the immortality and eternal life of man."

God Himself has a purpose. And His purpose revolves around you. If God's eternal work is centered on helping you grow, progress, and return to Him, then surely your life's purpose must also be tied to becoming something greater and helping others do the same.

Your purpose is your personal participation in God's work.

Read that again: Your purpose, no matter what it is, will be the way that you participate in God's purpose.

It might look like:

- Building a family where faith thrives.
- Teaching others with patience and joy.
- Creating beauty that lifts souls.
- Healing wounds—physical, emotional, or spiritual.
- Defending truth and light in a world growing increasingly dark.
- Stabilizing individuals and families.
- Developing structure for others to thrive.

Whatever your specific mission is, it will always connect back to bringing light, hope, and goodness into the world—and leading souls, including your own, back to Him. Remember what we learned earlier about outward focus—purpose always exists to serve a greater good.

In fact, some of the greatest unhappiness you will experience in this life will come from the pursuit of self-serving goals. You'll pour endless effort and focus into achieving them, only to discover that your house, bank account, and garage are full but your bucket is still empty.

Why We Struggle to Feel Purposeful

If knowing your purpose is so essential, why does it feel so hard to grasp sometimes?

Because we live in a mortal world filled with:

- Noise: Every voice around you (and inside your own head) is telling you what you should do, who you should be, and how you should live.

- Comparison: Social media makes it dangerously easy to measure your worth against curated images of other people's highlight reels.
- Busyness: Constant demands on your time can crowd out reflection, prayer, and the quiet spaces where God speaks.
- Pain: Trauma, disappointment, and failure can make you question your worth and your ability to make a difference.

All these forces create what I call Purpose Fog—a hazy, confusing atmosphere that makes it hard to see your divine direction clearly. But fog doesn't erase the road. It only obscures it for a time.

The path God placed you on is still there—solid and real—even when the mist around you feels thick and disorienting. Our job is to keep walking in faith until the next step becomes clear.

Clues to Your Purpose Are Already Within You

Here's something that might surprise you: You already have all the raw materials you need to understand your purpose.

It's not about chasing something brand-new. Your purpose isn't "out there" somewhere waiting to be tripped over. It's about noticing what God has already been weaving into your life from the beginning.

Some clues include:

- What you love naturally: What activities, topics, or causes make you feel most alive?
- Where you excel effortlessly: What strengths and skills do you seem to have an instinct for?
- What breaks your heart: What injustices, needs, or hurts stir deep emotion in you?
- What hardships you've survived: What pain have you endured that has shaped your compassion, resilience, or wisdom?

I often ask coaching clients to finish these simple sentences:

- "I feel most alive when I __________."
- "People often come to me for help with __________."
- "If I could fix one problem in the world, it would be __________."

- "When I was a kid, I dreamed of ___________."

Your answers to those questions aren't random. They are fingerprints of your divine mission. We'll discuss this even more in depth in the next few chapters, including concrete examples, but I want you to start considering that God has already planted clues in you to help you gain this clarity. He wants you to feel like you have direction!

A few months back, I was listening to a podcast interview with Brad Wilcox, former counselor in the General Young Men's Presidency of the Church and a current professor at Brigham Young University (BYU). Stephen Jones led the interview, and I heard a beautiful and simple example of clarified purpose in a story Brother Wilcox recounted.[18]

He talked about an experience many years ago when he met the then-prophet, President Spencer W. Kimball. Brother Wilcox was part of a cast of performers for "My Turn on Earth" in Salt Lake, and they got notice that President Kimball and his family would be in attendance. He was teaching Sunday School at the time and asked the youth what they would say to President Kimball if they had the chance to meet him. One boy would ask if the prophet knew how to water-ski, and another commented that he'd like to know if they wear makeup in general conference. One girl said she'd just tell him she loves him.

So the next night, after the performance, they took the small cast to meet President Kimball before he got in his car. The prophet asked Brother Wilcox what his calling was in the Church at the time and what he had taught the youth the day before. Brother Wilcox told him about his lesson with the youth, that the youth said they loved him, and that he loved him.

President Kimball then did something surprising. He wrapped his arms around Brother Wilcox and held him—not just hugged him but *held him*. And he said he'd never forget that experience. He then said, "I think that was one of the experiences that helped me find one of my missions in life. *It's to love.* And it's to try to let people feel the Savior's love by saying 'I love you' when they live in a world where their fathers and so many people that should say those words just don't. But it's one of the reasons I was born, and it was President Kimball who taught me that" (emphasis added).

No experience in life is wasted, and each has the potential to reveal your greater purpose. Since then, Brother Wilcox has used that simple purpose to align his actions in his career, family, and callings in the Church. "I exist to love." Purpose brings clarity and direction.

Your life experiences reveal your purpose, and once you know your purpose, you can devote your life to aligning your day-to-day actions to fulfill it, as Brother Wilcox has.

God's Pattern for Purpose Discovery

Throughout scripture, we see a beautiful, consistent pattern for how God reveals purpose to His children:

1. He plants a desire.
2. He prepares through experiences, oftentimes difficult.
3. He reveals through small moments of inspiration.
4. He empowers through covenants and grace.

Think about Moses.

Before he led Israel out of Egypt, he lived as a prince—learning leadership. Then as a shepherd—learning patience. Then as a prophet—learning to trust revelation.

Each season seemed disconnected at first. But in hindsight, it was obvious: God was shaping him for his purpose all along.

The same is true for you. No season is meaningless. No trial is pointless. God is always preparing you—even when you can't see it yet.

Living Purposefully Even When You Feel Small

Sometimes, even after you catch glimpses of your purpose, you'll still feel small.

You'll still wonder:

- Does this even matter?
- Am I making any difference at all?
- Wouldn't someone else do this better?

Let me be clear: Living your purpose doesn't always feel glamorous.

It often looks like small, repeated acts of obedience, love, and perseverance.

It looks like:

- Listening patiently to a lonely neighbor.
- Changing a diaper at 2 a.m. without resentment.
- Writing the first rough draft of a book no one has asked for—yet.
- Bearing your testimony in sacrament meeting even when your hands shake.
- Staying kind in a workplace that feels hostile.

Heaven doesn't measure greatness the way the world does. Purpose isn't about the size of your audience. It's about the size of your willingness.

President Dallin H. Oaks taught, "The final judgment is not just a summation of good and evil acts—what we have done. It is based on the final effect of our acts and thoughts—what we have become."[19]

Purpose isn't something you "achieve" once and for all.

It's something you become—little by little, grace by grace.

Purpose in Hidden Seasons

There will be seasons when your purpose feels obvious—when doors swing open and blessings pour down.

But there will also be seasons when it feels hidden—when progress is invisible, when prayers seem unanswered, when it takes every ounce of faith to keep moving forward.

Don't be discouraged by the hidden seasons.

Remember the parable of the seed planted in the earth.

Growth happens underground long before it bursts into view.

When you continue nurturing your faith, serving others, and living with integrity even when no one sees, you are living your purpose powerfully. President Dieter F. Uchtdorf beautifully reassures:

> God will take you as you are at this very moment and begin to work with you. All you need is a willing heart, a desire to believe, and trust in the Lord. Gideon saw himself as a poor farmer, the least

of his father's house. But God saw him as a mighty man of valor. When Samuel chose Saul to be king, Saul tried to talk him out of it. Saul was from one of the smallest tribes of the house of Israel. How could he be king? But God saw him as "a choice young man." Even the great prophet Moses felt so overwhelmed and discouraged at one point that he wanted to give up and die. But God did not give up on Moses.

My dear brothers and sisters, if we look at ourselves only through our mortal eyes, we may not see ourselves as good enough. But our Heavenly Father sees us as who we truly are and who we can become. He sees us as His sons and daughters, as beings of eternal light with everlasting potential and with a divine destiny.[20]

A Preview of What's Ahead

In this chapter, we've explored:

- Why purpose matters spiritually, emotionally, and physically.
- How God's eternal plan includes a personalized mission for you.
- The common reasons purpose feels confusing—and why that's normal.
- Practical steps to begin uncovering the divine fingerprints already in your life.

But we're just getting started.
In the chapters that follow, you'll learn how to:

- Dig into your past experiences through the Journey Map.
- Create a clear and inspiring personal purpose statement.
- Overcome the "villains" that try to keep you small.
- Build a daily life that reflects your divine mission.
- Stay connected to personal revelation as your purpose evolves.

Your purpose is not something to be invented.
It's something to be remembered.

You already made promises before you came to earth. You already carry within you the seeds of a great and holy work. Now—with faith, courage, and a willing heart—it's time to uncover them and live them out.

Are you ready?
Let's do it.

Reflection Exercise: Your Purpose Clues

Take a journal or notebook and write down honest answers to the following:

- What have been the most joyful experiences of your life?
- What challenges have left a permanent mark on your heart?
- What are you naturally good at—even when you don't try hard?
- What compliments do you frequently receive from others?
- If money, fear, and time weren't factors, how would you spend your days?
- What kinds of people or causes do you feel called to serve?

Sit with these questions.
Pray over them.
Ask Heavenly Father to open your heart and help you notice what He's already placed inside of you.
Remember, discovering your purpose isn't about forcing answers.
It's about noticing the answers that are already there.

2
How Do You Find Your Purpose?

"You were born with potential. You were born with goodness and trust. You were born with ideals and dreams. You were born with greatness. You were born with wings. You are not meant for crawling, so don't. You have wings. Learn to use them and fly." —Rumi[21]

Finding your purpose sounds so monumental, doesn't it?

As if it's a single golden scroll tucked away in a hidden temple, and your job is to go on a heroic quest to unearth it. It's no wonder so many people feel overwhelmed or discouraged by the idea. In fact, google "finding purpose is a waste of time" and count the number of videos, blog posts, and articles that pop up, such as "Why 'find your purpose' is bad advice and what to do instead."

We imagine that discovering our purpose requires a flash of divine revelation—a burning bush, a thunderous voice from the heavens, a neon sign flashing THIS WAY.

But in reality, purpose rarely arrives all at once. More often, it's revealed gradually, like the rising sun illuminating the landscape a little more each moment.

And the good news?

You don't have to wander aimlessly. There is a clear, simple process for uncovering your God-given purpose, one that has worked for the more than 2,000 people I've coached in one-on-one and large group settings in the past ten years.

It begins with a new understanding:

Purpose is discovered, not decided.

Myth: "You Must Invent Your Purpose"

One of the greatest lies of modern culture is the idea that you must invent yourself—that you must somehow conjure your meaning out of thin air, independent of anything or anyone else.

This sounds empowering at first: "You can be anything you want to be!" "Just follow your passion!"

But here's the problem: What if you don't know what your passion is yet? What if you have multiple interests and talents? What if the path you thought you wanted turns out to be empty?

Trying to invent your purpose without divine guidance is like trying to assemble a puzzle without knowing what the final picture looks like.

It leads to confusion. Frustration. Burnout.

God's way is different. You are not a random accident, scrambling to create a life worth living. You are a created being—designed with intention, skill, and love.

Your purpose was planted in you long before you were born.

Your job isn't to invent it. Your job is to uncover it—like an archaeologist brushing away layers of dust to reveal something ancient, sacred, and priceless.

The Three Characteristics of True Purpose

Through years of coaching thousands of people—young and old, seekers and leaders—I've found that true, lasting, God-centered purpose always has three essential characteristics:

- It's broad.
- It's short.

- It's influenced by your past.

Let's break these down one at a time.

1. It's Broad

If I were to ask you to play marketing professional for a moment and come up with a one-sentence, fifteen-word-or-less purpose statement for why each of these organizations exists, what would you say?

- Disney
- Amazon
- Tesla

In my years running this activity, I usually get a few cynics who come up with things like "to make money at the expense of their customers" or "to conquer the world." Although possibly true, I'll forgo commenting on these statements for now. In fact, below are their purpose statements, directly from their websites:

- Disney: To make people happy.
- Amazon: To be the earth's most customer-centric company.
- Tesla: To accelerate the world's transition to sustainable energy.

Typically, when I share these with the group, I get laughter, a few guffaws, and some subtle remarks like "Have you ever *been* to Disney with kids on a hot Friday afternoon? Nothing happy about it!" While that may be true, this brings up a few important aspects of purpose. What do you notice they all have in common?

First, they're idealistic. They are big, broad statements that could never be accomplished in a lifetime. They aren't quantitatively measurable, they lack specifics, and if I were to remove the names of the companies, these statements could just as easily be attributed to a grocery chain, car dealership, or restaurant. And that's the point. Purpose is the "why," and it's big, bold, broad, and, therefore, motivating.

If we were to look at Disney, their purpose is to make people happy, their "how" is through entertainment and media, and their "what" is through merchandise, parks, movies, and channels. If a grocery chain used that same "why"—to make people happy—their "how" might be through food, and their "what" could be name-brand products at low prices. In other words, purpose statements are broad and should say nothing about your specific talents or goals.

In fact, your purpose should be so broad that you could never accomplish it in a lifetime. Think about these purpose statements:

- God's purpose: "This is my work and my glory—*to bring to pass the immortality and eternal life of man*." (Moses 1:39)
- Our purpose: "Behold, this is your work, *to keep my commandments*, yea, with all your might, mind and strength." (Doctrine and Covenants 11:20)
- The purpose of The Church of Jesus Christ of Latter-day Saints:
- *To develop* in people's lives *Christlike attributes.*
- *Transform society* so that the world may be a better and more peaceful place in which to live.22
- The purpose of the Relief Society (2017): Help *prepare women for the blessings of eternal life.*23

Are these quantifiable? Not in the near-term. Are they broad? Oh yeah. HUGE. But that's what makes them motivating. It's what causes people to strive to bring them to pass.

What's your purpose? Whatever it is, it should be broad.

Your purpose isn't meant to be narrow or restrictive.

It's not about locking yourself into one career, one city, one ministry, or one fixed identity.

Rather, true purpose is expansive—it can be expressed in dozens of different ways across the seasons of your life.

Think about the Savior's earthly mission. He healed the sick. He taught the multitudes. He wept with the grieving. He washed the feet of His disciples.

His purpose—to bring about the immortality and eternal life of mankind—was carried out in countless diverse actions.

Your life will be similar.

You might live your purpose:

- As a parent nurturing faith at the kitchen table
- As an entrepreneur creating opportunities for others
- As a teacher sparking a love of learning

- As a quiet friend standing beside someone in grief

The expressions of your purpose may change, but the essence of it will stay true.

2. It's Short

Second, purpose statements are short. How short? This short:

- To help people be their best selves.
- To pursue knowledge to share with others.
- To create systems that make life easier.
- To find order in chaos.
- To close the gap!
- To springboard people forward.

These actual purpose statements from past clients have one important thing in common: They're ten words or less. Great purpose statements are concise and to the point.

Why is that?

A few years ago, I was coaching a friend who asked me to review his purpose statement. When he sent it to me, it was more like a narrative. It was a full page, single-spaced. To be fair, it was a very visionary and motivating purpose. It read something like "I exist to find ways to serve people to help them to rise above their past experiences and difficulties and to become someone greater than . . . " and then I can't recall the rest. In fact, he couldn't remember it either. I called him up and asked him to share his purpose with me from memory, and he got lost around halfway through the first sentence.

My challenge to him was the same one I'd give you: Keep it short. I'd recommend around ten words, including the intro, "I exist to . . . ," because the great truth is that if you can't remember it, it holds no power. If you can't roll out of bed in the morning, plant your feet on the floor, and repeat your purpose to yourself to start your day, you're missing the motivating factor.

Your purpose statement isn't supposed to be a paragraph. It's not a personal essay or a résumé summary. It's a battle cry. Something so clear and compact you could carry it into a meeting, a prayer, or a hard conversation and know exactly who you are and why you're there. The goal isn't to explain everything. The goal is to anchor you—fast.

Remember the purpose I came up with when I was curled up on the living room floor? *To maximize human potential.* Boom. That's it. Those four words have become my North Star, and each word is intentional and holds power. The same should be true for you. When you only get ten words or less, you can't afford fluff or ambiguous language. Make every word count. Do you *drive* change? Why not inspire it, catalyze it, or empower it? Are you all about *building* people? Why not growing them, developing them, or motivating them? Choose your words wisely and remember to keep it short.

When your life gets busy or hard or loud (and it will), you won't have time to dig through three journal pages trying to remember what God called you to do. You'll need something you can say in a single breath. Ten words or less. Short enough to memorize. Sharp enough to cut through the fog. Think of it like a spiritual compass—the simpler it is, the more likely you are to use it.

It should be memorable, and the way to make it memorable is to keep it concise.

If your purpose is a sword, brevity sharpens the blade.

3. It's Influenced by Your Past

This has been perhaps the greatest finding and "aha moment" I've discovered about purpose: It's not out there in the future, waiting to be discovered. It's in your past. It's in the rearview mirror. Purpose is behind you, waiting to be mined, not in front of you, waiting for you to stumble across it!

Let me explain.

Anytime I'm coaching a person on identifying their purpose, I have them get out a blank sheet of paper and draw a squiggly line horizontally from left to right, up and down across the page. It ends up looking like a stock ticker or a roller coaster.

I explain to my client that this line should represent the highs and lows of their life. Each individual will do the activity slightly differently, and that's okay. They'll chart their life, then label the peaks and valleys, such as "graduating from college" or "losing my job" or, for me, "making Beano calls." (That would be a low—like, the ultimate valley.)

The key is to capture the peaks and valleys of life. Thus far, I haven't met a client with only peaks or valleys. Most have lived a life that looks something like a rollercoaster ride.

Why is this line so important?

The key to this line is that your purpose lies somewhere along the journey.

In 2007, a group of leadership researchers led by Bill George published some interesting findings.[24] They diagrammed the leadership trajectory of 125 leaders from twenty-three to ninety-three years old and found that leaders experienced highs and lows along their journey that helped them form their character, drove them to lead, and ultimately led them to step into peak leadership. Even more interestingly, most often their peak levels of leadership emerged sometime around mid-life from what they termed their "crucibles," or those low moments in life. In other words, their lows made them who they are.

By the way, I love the word "crucible" as a descriptor of those lows. A crucible is a severe test or trial that reveals and refines what something is truly made of. In ancient metallurgy, a crucible was a heat-resistant container used to melt and purify metals, separating out the impurities so only the strongest material remained. Spiritually or personally, a crucible refers to intense experiences—suffering, pressure, loss, uncertainty—that burn away what's shallow and force you to confront what's real.

Crucibles don't create purpose, but they clarify it. They strip away the noise and force you to ask, "Who am I really? What do I actually believe? What still matters when everything else falls away?"

As I pondered this research, the thought hit me that purpose also emerges from the highs and lows of life. Sometimes we have a high experience—a peak—that causes us to say, "Wow! I want everyone to experience this. I want to spend my life helping people have this experience." Other times we experience hard lows that make us step back and say, "Man, I don't want anyone to experience what I went through. I exist to ensure no one is alone."

In either case, purpose is driven by the past, not the future. We're motivated to make changes in the world because of what we've experienced, for better or worse.

Can purpose emerge from either? The highs or the lows? The answer is yes, although unsurprisingly I would say that, anecdotally, 90 percent of the time, the people I coach discover their purpose from the lows of life. When we experience something hard, difficult, or traumatic, we tend to feel motivated to create change in the world so that others don't walk the same path.

That said, I once coached a guy who said, "Dustin, I simply haven't experienced many lows in my life." For him, his purpose emerged from his highs—those moments when he was satisfied, motivated, energized, and on fire. He wanted to spend his life helping others experience the same.

Purpose comes from the past, not the future. Let me give an example.

Sydney's Story

I get about three to five random emails a week from people I've never met who want to learn more about how to reset their careers. I've come to expect them, and if a week were to pass without my random cadre of emails, I'm not sure what I'd do. Sydney's message was one of those.

Sydney reached out after having bought my book and wanted to talk more about assisting her with her transition.

I was particularly interested in meeting Sydney because she was a nontraditional client. After some basic research, I learned that she owned her own media company, lived in a high-rise, and was late in her career, perhaps in her late fifties. And yet she was also wanting to reset.

We set up a time, and I met her at her place. Sydney is sharp and buttoned up. She'd had an extensive career in oil and gas and had left her work to be at home with their young daughter. She wanted to find something meaningful to do—a passion—and was open to feedback and help.

I asked Sydney to map her life, and particularly her work experience, to show the highs and lows—the moments when she thrived and languished. We then talked it through, and as usually occurs when people talk through where they've come from, her purpose emerged.

Her highs were all moments when she was on her game, well-respected by her colleagues and superiors, and brought in to do a specific work that only she could do. Her lows were quite the opposite. She described moments when she felt disrespected, disempowered, and lacking the confidence to advocate for herself.

As we spoke, she teared up, remembering the pain of those lows.

When we emerged from the discussion, I reflected back to her what I heard and said, "If you could spend the rest of your life doing one thing, what would it be?"

"Helping others find their voice, feel empowered and confident, and advocate for their needs," she said.

This is the start of a purpose. For Sydney, it was clear—she wants to help women in their careers figure out how to advocate for what they want. Where did this come from? Her own experience. It always does.

Purpose is our desire to affect others and the world we live in in a way that creates lasting impact. It's that thing that lights your fire. It's the target at which you can aim your talents.

Passion—which is what most people talk about—is the *emotional* side of purpose, meaning passion and purpose are directly connected. Purpose is your "why," and passion is the associated emotional instinct that drives you.

Purpose isn't "out there" somewhere in the future. In fact, it's in you . . . and it's in the past. Purpose emerges from the highs and lows of your life, and most often (again, 90 percent of the time) from the lows. Crucible moments define who we are, and we often emerge on the other side of them saying, "If I could spend the rest of my life making sure no one ever feels like I would, I'd do it in a heartbeat." That's purpose. And that's what drives me.

You don't find your purpose by staring into the clouds or guessing at the future. You find it by examining the life you've already lived. Your past experiences—the joys, the pains, the triumphs, the heartbreaks—are not random. They are preparation.

God has been shaping you, crafting you, refining you for your mission long before you were even aware of it.

Think about it:

- Joseph of Egypt's betrayal, slavery, and imprisonment prepared him to save nations during a famine.
- Esther's grace, wisdom, and position as queen prepared her to deliver her people from destruction.
- Alma the Younger's rebellious past gave him unique empathy and passion as a missionary to the wayward.

Your story matters. Not just the shiny parts but especially the broken ones. Your scars are signposts. Your struggles are training grounds. Your history holds the keys to your destiny.

Purpose Hidden in Plain Sight

Let me tell you about a few other people I've worked with—people just like you, who initially felt lost or overwhelmed when it came to finding their purpose.

Their stories show that purpose is almost always hiding in plain sight, tucked inside the experiences you already carry.

Karla's Story: From Outsider to Advocate

When Karla came to me, she was frustrated.

"I just don't know if I'm doing anything that matters," she said. "I'm volunteering at a nonprofit, but it feels . . . hollow."

We dug into her life story, and something quickly emerged: As a teenager, Karla had fought to stay in school after facing discrimination. She knew what it felt like to be marginalized, overlooked, underestimated.

Her greatest pain had created her greatest passion: helping others find their voice.

Today, Karla leads programs that empower underrepresented youth to advocate for themselves. Her purpose statement became "To amplify the voices of the unseen."

Mark's Story: Healing Through Compassion

Mark was a medical student feeling burned out.

"I thought becoming a doctor would be my purpose," he confessed, "but now it just feels like an endless grind."

We reviewed the highs and lows of his life.

One experience stood out sharply: a long hospitalization during his teenage years where he felt isolated and invisible to the hospital staff.

That season of suffering gave Mark a deep well of compassion.

We reframed his calling: He wasn't just meant to treat symptoms. He was meant to heal people's sense of dignity.

Mark's purpose became "To see and soothe the overlooked."

Your Story: Hidden Clues Waiting to Surface

You might not realize it yet, but your life holds similar clues.

The wounds you carry? The battles you've fought? The causes that make your heart ache or your spirit ignite?

They're not random. They're invitations—whispering the shape of your divine mission.

But they require you to slow down, notice, and listen.

Reflection Exercise: Finding Purpose Clues

Grab a journal and spend some time answering these questions:

- What have been the three most joyful moments of my life so far?
- What have been the three most painful moments?
- What strengths did I develop because of those painful experiences?
- When do I feel most "at home"—most myself?
- If I could solve one problem in the world, what would it be?

Take your time. Don't rush. These questions aren't busywork—they are sacred excavation. What you find buried beneath the surface could change everything.

Listening for the Still, Small Voice

Discovering your purpose is not just an intellectual exercise. It's a spiritual process. The Spirit speaks quietly—almost imperceptibly—but with unmistakable truth when you learn how to listen. When pondering your past, your passions, your pains, invite the Spirit into the process.

Pray specifically: "Heavenly Father, help me see the purpose Thou hast planted in me. Show me where I can do the most good. Reveal the gifts Thou hast given me to serve others."

Then pay attention to:

- The ideas that persist in your mind
- The nudges you feel to serve or create
- The gentle excitement when you imagine certain paths
- The scripture verses or talks that suddenly feel personal

Finding your purpose is not something you can do on your own strength. It requires divine partnership.

And God is eager—absolutely eager—to reveal it to you.

You are His work. You are His glory.

And He wants you to know exactly why He sent you here.

Taking Action—Even Before You Feel "Ready"

One of the greatest mistakes people make when seeking their purpose is waiting for complete clarity before taking action.

They think:

- "I'll move forward once I'm 100% sure."
- "I need a full blueprint before I start."
- "What if I pick the wrong thing?"

But here's the truth:

Clarity comes through movement, not just meditation. This means that while thinking, praying, and pondering are valuable, true understanding often comes when we act, not just when we sit and reflect. Insight is often found in the process of doing rather than waiting for perfect answers beforehand. For example, a college student unsure of which major to choose might never gain clarity just by pondering.

But by taking introductory classes, talking to professionals, or doing internships, they begin to sense what fits—and clarity comes through that experience. Or a person debating whether to serve a mission or take a job might not receive a clear answer in prayer immediately. But once they start preparing for the mission—speaking with leaders, saving money, submitting paperwork—direction often becomes more evident. Likewise, a woman feeling prompted to switch careers may not receive detailed instructions from God while waiting at home. But once she begins networking, applying, or updating her skills, doors begin to open that she hadn't expected.

God directs our steps as we walk, not as we sit paralyzed by indecision.

Think about Nephi. When Nephi and his brothers were commanded to return to Jerusalem to obtain the brass plates from Laban, the task seemed daunting and dangerous. Their first attempts failed, and the situation grew more uncertain. Nephi could have parked himself in the tent to wait for his next step from God. He might have pulled out a scroll to concept map his options. Or he could have slept on it, figuring a good night's sleep might resolve the dilemma. Yet Nephi remained faithful and willing to act, even without knowing the outcome. Rather than waiting for a detailed plan or perfect conditions, he moved forward with trust in the Lord. His experience teaches a powerful principle: that guidance often comes after we begin to act in faith. As Nephi himself testified, "I was led by the Spirit, not knowing beforehand the things which I should do" (1 Nephi 4:6). He moved forward with faith—and the way opened, one step at a time.

The same principle applies to discovering your purpose.

You don't have to wait for a flashing neon sign. You don't have to sit on the sidelines until everything feels perfect. Start where you are. Take the next faithful step.

Faithful Small Steps Toward Purpose

Here are simple, faith-filled actions you can take today to begin aligning your life more fully with your purpose:

- Serve where you are. Opportunities to fulfill your mission often begin with simple acts of kindness right in front of you.

- Create something. Write, build, teach, heal, mentor, nurture. Creation is an expression of divine identity.
- Say yes to small promptings. If you feel nudged to reach out to someone, volunteer, study a topic, or apply for a role—do it.
- Stay curious. Explore interests without demanding they immediately reveal your life's calling.
- Trust the unfolding. Believe that God reveals your path in layers—exactly when you're ready to receive them.

Purpose isn't something you find once and then coast forever. It's a relationship—a continual conversation with God as you grow, learn, and serve.

What to Expect as You Step Forward

When you begin acting with intention, two things happen:

- Confirmation. You'll feel peace, excitement, and a sense of "rightness" when you're moving in alignment with your divine design. Doors will begin to open. Synchronicities will multiply.
- Correction. Sometimes you'll start down a path and realize it's not quite right. That's okay. Redirection is part of revelation. God honors your willingness and guides your course.

Moving with faith is never wasted.

Even if you don't land exactly where you thought you would, you will be closer to the person God is shaping you to become.

Final Reflection: Faith in the Journey

Finding your purpose is not about unlocking one big secret.

It's about walking with God, day by day, and letting Him teach you who you really are.

It's about trusting that you're not lost. You are not forgotten. You are on sacred ground—even when it feels ordinary.

The poet Mary Oliver once asked, "Tell me, what is it you plan to do with your one wild and precious life?"

The Lord asks you a deeper version of that question: "What will you do with the gifts I have entrusted to you? With the experiences I have prepared you through? With the heart I have shaped for this exact time in the world?"

You don't have to have every answer yet.

You just have to say, "Here I am, Lord. Use me."

And then—step by step, moment by moment—your purpose will unfold like the sunrise, filling your life and the lives of others with light.

3
The Journey Map: Mining Your Past for Purpose

"The past is never dead. It's not even past." —William Faulkner[25]

"Remember the worth of souls is great in the sight of God." —Doctrine and Covenants 18:10

Several years ago, I was asked to speak to a group of 250 first-year medical students as part of a wellness program. The topic was open. I was simply tasked with speaking about something that would help them as they set out on a massive journey of schooling, residency, high-pressure situations, testing, and financial load that would eventually be relieved sometime in their late thirties. I think the exact invitation from my client was "Speak about whatever you want . . . something 'leadershippy.'"

Yikes. I had no idea where to start. I knew nothing about medicine except how to use it to cure a headache. I had used doctors and medicine before but otherwise knew very little about what their experience must be as medical students.

I wasn't sure what to teach, but three days before the gig, the answer came.

My friend and neighbor, Keith, had dropped by to deliver some treats his wife had made. Keith is an anesthesiologist by trade, and we often talked about the power of finding your purpose.

After dropping off the treats, and as Keith got ready to leave, a Texas rainstorm kicked up, making it hard to walk down the street to his house. I offered to drive him, figuring he'd have some advice for what I might say. We got in the car, and I got right to the point.

"What do you wish you'd known when you started medical school?" I asked.

He thought about it and then said, "If there's one thing you can teach these students that will have the biggest impact on their journey through medical school, teach them their 'why.' I wish I had known my purpose."

I asked him to explain.

He told me about his two-year-old daughter, Evelyn. Our family knew "Eve" well because she was an escape artist who loved my wife. She'd break free from her house and wander down to our house, ringing the doorbell a dozen times or smashing her face against the glass door looking for "mommy Samye." She especially loved our dog "Lucy," but only at arm's length.

One morning, Eve woke up and became interested in her IKEA nightlight in her room. She pulled it from the wall, deconstructed it, and found a small, round disc—a battery. Any guess what she did with it? If you guessed "ate it," you must know kids. She stuck it in her mouth and swallowed it—except the battery became lodged in her throat.

She began to cry, and her parents rushed in. Recognizing that she was in significant pain, and putting the pieces together, they realized what she'd done and took her to the emergency room. They x-rayed her and saw the small, disc-shaped battery stuck in her throat. What's worse, it was leaking acid and eroding her esophagus. If it stayed much longer, it would burn right through.

At this point, Keith paused. "I felt helpless," he said, obviously reliving the moment in his mind. Despite his many years of training, this felt different. His sweet daughter was experiencing a potentially life-altering trauma.

Thankfully, they did an emergency procedure on her and extracted it successfully, and she began the process of healing. If it had stayed in her throat another hour, it might have been devastating.

"Wow," I said. "What a blessing that she was okay. So what does that have to do with your purpose?"

"In that moment," he said, "I would have done anything to help my daughter. It was a helpless feeling standing on the sidelines and seeing her go through that. Now, as an anesthesiologist, I often think about that experience when I'm helping patients. I'll think to myself, 'That's someone's Eve.' For example, I was recently on a pediatrics rotation, and I saw every kid in there as someone's child. I don't ever want a parent—or child for that matter—to feel what I felt."

"Is that only for kids?" I asked.

"Not at all. In fact, I've seen people come in chained to their beds by handcuffs with a police escort. Some people might be tempted to say 'I wonder what they did . . .' and treat them differently. But to me, in that moment, that's someone's Eve. That's someone's kid. And they're worthy of the same treatment that my daughter received that day."

Keith's core purpose could be summarized in three words: "That's someone's Eve."

He exists to heal people. He's all about making sure a parent doesn't feel what he felt: helpless. Keith's about confident care, and that core purpose motivated him when residency got tough.

His "how" and "what" may change, but his "why" remains consistent. Whether he's interacting with someone at church, in his family, or in the community, he strives to see people as they are—someone's child, and especially as a child of God.

In *Man's Search for Meaning*, Viktor Frankl said this: "A man who becomes conscious of the responsibility he bears toward a human being who affectionately waits for him, or to an unfinished work, will never be able to throw away his life. He knows the 'why' for his existence and will be able to bear almost any 'how.'"[26]

That's the power of purpose: It's a motivator. It guides us and keeps us grinding toward a better life for ourselves and those around us. Purpose is the ultimate North Star.

So what's your purpose? What's the deep reason for your existence, the driving force that motivates you?

Remember, the key to identifying purpose lies in the past, not the future.

Let me say that again, because it's the key to discovering purpose. Your purpose and passion aren't "out there" somewhere, waiting to be discovered. They're in your past, waiting to be uncovered.

Finding your purpose doesn't require peering into a crystal ball or obsessing over the distant future.

In fact, some of the strongest, clearest clues to your purpose aren't in your future. They're right behind you.

They're embedded in the life you've already lived—in the victories you've celebrated, the trials you've endured, and the ways you've been shaped, even when you didn't realize it.

In this chapter, we're going to uncover your purpose by mining the treasure already hidden inside your past.

How?

With a simple but powerful tool called the Journey Map. Similar to the up-and-down line I alluded to in chapter 2 that I have my coaching clients draw, the Journey Map is a structured exercise to gain clarity and mine purpose.

Your Life Is Not Random

Before we dive into the Journey Map, I need you to hear something—not just with your ears but with your soul:

Nothing in your life has been random or useless. Not a single tear. Not a single joy. Not a single heartbreak, mistake, or delay.

Every experience you've had—the ones you cherish and the ones you'd rather forget—has been allowed by a loving Father in Heaven to shape you, refine you, and prepare you for the mission He sent you here to fulfill.

Sometimes in the middle of suffering, it's easy to think, "This can't possibly have a purpose. This part of my story must have been a mistake."

But God is a master craftsman. He wastes nothing. He weaves everything—even the broken threads—into a tapestry of divine design.

As the Apostle Paul taught, "And we know that all things work together for good to them that love God, to them who are the called according to his purpose" (Romans 8:28).

When you begin to see your life through this lens—not as a random series of events but as a sacred preparation—you unlock a powerful truth: Your past holds the map to your future.

According to Bill Damon, purpose is often discovered not in a lightning bolt but in reflection—by looking back over your experiences and recognizing where meaning has consistently emerged.[27] It's in reviewing what you've cared about, what you've overcome, and where you've felt most alive that patterns begin to form.

Introducing the Journey Map

As I mentioned at the beginning of this section, one of the best activities I've used in coaching to help people get clear about their purpose is the Journey Map. As you get clear about the defining moments in your life that have shaped who you are, consistent themes emerge that give you clues about your values, strengths, and ideal environments for thriving. The Journey Map is a visual tool that helps you plot the key moments of your life so that you can see patterns, themes, and divine fingerprints you might have missed.

It's simple. It's powerful. And for many people, it's transformational.

Here's what it looks like in practice.

How to Create Your Journey Map

1. Grab a sheet of paper and turn it horizontally.
2. Draw a horizontal line across the center of the paper from left to right. This line represents your life timeline—from birth until today. It's also your baseline. Draw a vertical line at the left edge of

the paper and label the top of that line "10" and the bottom of the line "0." This is a sort of scale of happiness or joy.

3. Now mark significant events above or below the center line. For now, you might just plot them with dots and descriptors. Above the line, place the high points—moments of joy, success, breakthroughs, connection. Below the line, place the low points—moments of pain, loss, failure, grief.
4. Label each point with a word or short phrase. For example, "Baptized at 8," "Moved across the country," "Lost a parent," "Started my own business," "Overcame addiction."
5. Connect the dots. Step back and look at the pattern. Notice the arcs, dips, and rises. Pay attention to recurring themes.
6. By the way, there is no one "right" way that this should look. I've had some clients throw it in a spreadsheet and others draw it with markers on paper. Each scale might look different. Don't overthink it. The goal is to have a rollercoaster-like line—labeled—representing the highs and lows of your life from birth to today.
7. Reflect deeply. Pick a moment that stands out—a high or a low—and ask the following questions:

    - What lessons emerged from this peak/valley?
    - What difficulty did I experience that I want to solve for others?
    - Why was that moment significant? What did I learn about myself?
    - As a result of experiencing that thing, what problem do I want to solve in the world? What impact do I hope to have?
    - What passions or talents surfaced during the peaks that I would want to make possible for others?
    - Where do I see the hand of God guiding, protecting, or preparing me?
    - If I had to summarize my takeaway from that experience in ten words or less, what would it be?
    - What clues did that experience give me about my purpose for existence?

Remember to look at both the highs and the lows because purpose can emerge from either. I once coached a guy who felt like he'd lived a pretty charmed life. He was afraid that his chart wouldn't have many lows and that he would be left without purpose. He was forty years old at the time, which is plenty of time to have established a life purpose. As we reviewed his map, it became clear that his purpose was tied to his highs, not his lows. He had experienced significant moments that he wanted to replicate for others. That became his purpose.

And yet, as discussed before, most of the time purpose emerges from the lows, not the highs. When you experience something low, deep, and painful, you often want to spend the rest of your life ensuring others don't experience what you went through.

When people begin mapping their life stories to uncover purpose, they often skip over the hard chapters. The betrayal. The addiction. The loss. The season of depression. The faith crisis. The failure that still stings when you speak it out loud.

We're conditioned to think purpose comes from success, from clarity and confidence and breakthrough moments. But Dr. Paul T. P. Wong—a clinical psychologist and pioneer in existential positive psychology—argues that we've been looking in the wrong place.[28]

According to Wong, meaning isn't something we find *after* the suffering is over. It's something we uncover *through* it.

He calls this "the positive psychology of suffering"—the idea that pain, when engaged with honestly, can lead to deep personal transformation and a renewed sense of purpose. Wong's work shows that people who have suffered deeply often become the very people who lead others through similar storms. Not because they're flawless or unscarred but because they found meaning in what nearly broke them.

This isn't self-help fluff. It's hard-won truth. Wong's research found that those who integrated their painful experiences—instead of avoiding them—actually reported greater levels of life satisfaction, purpose, and emotional resilience. They were more likely to engage in meaningful relationships and more likely to help others. Their suffering hadn't ruined them. It had refined them.

Wong calls this the path of self-transcendence—the ability to move beyond yourself, even your pain, and connect to something greater. That could be a cause, a community, a relationship, or faith in God. And this movement outward doesn't erase the suffering—it transforms it. The wound becomes the womb of something new.

This fits perfectly into your Journey Map.

When you sit down to trace your story, don't skip the parts that hurt. Pause there. Linger. Ask: What did I lose in this season—and what did I gain? What did I learn to value? What did I see more clearly about myself, about God, about the world? What changed in me that couldn't have happened any other way?

Your scars are not liabilities to your purpose. They're clues.

You're not defined by what you've been through, but you are shaped by how you respond to it. And the good news is that even in the darkest chapters, you were never alone. God was there. And He was planting something.

Wong once said, "Suffering is the price we pay for a meaningful life." That doesn't mean we chase pain. But it means we no longer run from it. We mine it. We let it shape us. We let it teach us how to live with compassion and conviction.

Because your pain—named, healed, and offered—might be the very thing that unlocks someone else's purpose too.

So look back at your map. Identify the highs and lows, then ask yourself a powerful question: "Why?" Why was the moment so significant? Why was it so low or so high? As with Keith and my own story, the answer to "why" often reveals your purpose.

Let me give another example. Several months ago, I coached Chris, a college senior who came to me to gain clarity about his career path. As we explored his journey through life, he became passionate about a story from his sophomore year of college.

Chris had sustained a puncture to his lungs in an accident that required him to be immediately hospitalized. As he lay in significant pain, hundreds of miles away from family, he felt alone. What's worse, he found the hospital staff and attending nurses to be generally lacking in empathy and emotional intelligence. The environment felt cold and sterile, which is good for cleanliness but bad for patient well-being. That moment had a significant effect on him.

He's now looking into internal medicine, with an emphasis in nursing, in order to provide an uplifting, caring, and supportive environment for trauma patients. His purpose? "Improve the quality of life of patients."

Talk It Out

One other key to uncovering your purpose is that it most often comes when you talk about it out loud with another person. I don't know why that is, but I've almost never met anyone who has clarified their purpose in isolation. It just doesn't come as you sit quietly in a room and ponder. There's something about speaking out loud and having another person hear you that brings it to a clear point.

However, the other person has a role as well. They're not there just to listen and affirm. They don't just smile and nod. Their job is to listen and ask why. Why does that moment stand out to you? Why did that impact you so much? Why does that matter? And at some point, they shift to questions like "What does that teach you about your purpose?" or "How did that shape who you are today?"

As you talk it out and have another person there to reflect back what they hear and ask questions, an interesting thing will happen. As you tell your story and they ask why over and over again, you'll eventually get to the point that your cheeks flush, you might get frustrated, and you'll proclaim, "I don't know why! I guess I just care about . . . *maximizing human potential.*" Or ". . . *healing suffering.*" Or ". . . *helping those who can't help themselves.*" Bam! Your purpose usually emerges as the last seven words you say. Right at the end of your narrative when you've talked through the difficulty and pain, or the joy and elation, you'll find yourself saying, "I guess I just care about ____________." And there it is.

This is the magic of the workshops we lead! People get a chance to pair up, share their story, and uncover the deeper meaning. That said, you don't need a workshop—find a friend, loved one, significant other, or mentor. Invite them to listen as you share your story, then pay attention to what you say.

By the way, how will you know when you've landed on your purpose? We'll talk about this more in depth in a moment, but the short answer is you should *feel it.* It should do something for you. Purpose is deeply personal and tied to your identity and life experience, so when you get there, it will move you.

Don't feel it when you say it? You may not be there yet. Again, more on this shortly.

The Refining Fire: On Suffering and Sanctification

When we talk about purpose, it's tempting to think only in terms of progress—forward momentum, clarity, achievement. But often the most defining moments of our lives come not when we're climbing the mountain but when we're face-down in the valley, wondering if we'll ever get up again.

Elder Neal A. Maxwell, who served in the Quorum of the Twelve Apostles, understood this on both a personal and theological level. Before his call to the apostleship, he battled leukemia. And from that place of physical suffering and spiritual clarity, he became one of the most powerful voices in the Church on the purpose of pain.

Elder Maxwell once said, "Sometimes the best people have the worst experiences because they are the most ready to learn."[29]

He taught that adversity isn't always a sign of being off track; sometimes it's proof that God is shaping something deeper within us. "If the Lord were to polish us with sandpaper," he said, "we must not mistake the process for the product."[30]

In other words, the pain you've walked through may not have been random. It may have been refining.

This fits hand-in-glove with the Journey Map. When we look back at our stories, we tend to skip the bruised parts—the failure, the heartbreak, the stretch of silence where we wondered if God had gone quiet. But those are often the places where identity is forged and purpose gets clarified.

Elder Maxwell described these moments not as detours but as "customized trials"—designed by a loving God who knows what our soul is being prepared for. He wrote, "The very act of choosing to trust Him in the face of unexplainable adversity is, in itself, a kind of consecration." That kind of trust—in the middle of pain—becomes the soil where purpose grows.

So when you're tracing your story, don't rush past the hard chapters. Sit with them. Ask God, "What were You trying to show me there? What in me were You trying to change, strengthen, or awaken?" You may find that the moments you resented are the very ones that prepared you for what comes next.

In the eyes of the world, suffering just slows you down. But in the eyes of God, suffering—*sanctified suffering*—is often where He does His most focused, most intimate work. Work that prepares you not just to live your purpose but to carry it with authority, with compassion, and with holy fire.

Example: Sarah's Journey Map

Let me share another real-world example.

Sarah, a client of mine, was in her early forties when she came to me feeling deeply unfulfilled.

"I feel like I've wasted so many years," she said through tears. "I don't even know who I am anymore."

I introduced her to the Journey Map exercise.

At first, she resisted. She was afraid to revisit painful memories—afraid the past would confirm her fears of failure.

But slowly, courageously, she began mapping:

- Age 8: Parents' divorce—deep feelings of abandonment
- Age 14: Winning a local writing competition—feeling seen and valued
- Age 19: Dropping out of college—feeling lost
- Age 23: Baptized into the Church—profound spiritual awakening
- Age 30: Becoming a mother—experiencing unconditional love
- Age 37: Launching a small blog—reconnecting to writing
- Age 40: Losing her father—wrestling with grief and legacy

When Sarah stepped back and looked at her map, she wept—not with sorrow but with awe. Through every twist and turn, a consistent thread had been running: healing through words.

Writing had always been her sanctuary—her way of making sense of the world, connecting with others, and finding healing for herself and others. Her pain wasn't pointless. Her delays weren't wasted. God had been guiding her all along.

Sarah's purpose emerged clearly: "To heal hearts through honest words."

She now writes full-time, mentoring others through grief and life transitions.

Her journey wasn't ruined. It was redeemed.

Why the Highs and Lows Matter Spiritually

It's tempting to think that only the good parts of our lives—the awards, the victories, the mountaintop moments—are useful to God.

But that's not true.

Both your highest joys and your deepest sorrows shape your divine purpose.

A while back, I got a message from my good buddy Bryce: "So you know that part of your book, RESET, when you talked about how you had the breakdown and were crying and told Samye that you hated your job? I had that this weekend. Total breakdown. I needed it. It was a game changer for Cassie and me. I don't think she's ever seen me like that."

As soon as I got this text, I called Bryce to find out more. It started the previous week when he was sitting at lunch with his colleagues in the construction industry and thought, "Man, what am I doing here?" It carried over to Friday when his manager told him he needed some additional training in executing home warranties, and she wanted to carve out some significant time to train him in that. Saturday, he felt it well up as he talked with some buddies at lunch about work, but he crashed on Sunday morning, crying in the closet before church.

This is the price of incongruence. You can only fake it for so long, convincing yourself that "It's a good company!" or "The benefits are worth it" or "They're paying for a trip to Maui next spring."

The good news is that hitting bottom is a crucial step. In the coaching world, it's called "felt need"—where the client feels the need to change.

Bryce knew he needed to change. He had talked about it, considered it, pondered it, and talked about it some more. But he didn't take action . . . until he did.

The day he and I talked, he was on his way to visit an old college professor to seek some advice about how to get back to where he was four years ago, his true purpose:

"I exist to facilitate healing in others."

Today, many years later, Bryce leads teams of healthcare workers to bring healing to those who need it most. He's living squarely in his purpose and is exceptional at it. The journey to arrive back at congruence wasn't easy, but it paid off, both temporally and spiritually.

Now for a warning about this Journey Map activity: Sometimes we don't want to explore those lows because they were too traumatic. I coached a client who said she'd experienced some abuse in her past that was too sensitive to explore. I understand and am not trained or qualified to help clients unpack those stories. That said, my purpose isn't always directly aligned with the low I experienced.

In other words, if you had a death in the family, that doesn't mean your purpose is to help people cope with death. If your parents divorced, you're not destined to be a divorce attorney or a marriage counselor. Purpose is not the same as industry or career. It's deeper than that, bigger than that. It's your big "why." I can have the same purpose as someone else and activate it in a very different way.

Take my purpose, for example. I choose to maximize human potential by career coaching and leadership training, but others with the same purpose might be doctors, teachers, financial coaches, athletic trainers, or other human-oriented professions. I also live my purpose as a husband and father, church leader, and community member. My purpose is manifest in my day-to-day work, but it exists beyond that as a greater driving force for everything I do.

So although the lows may be painful to explore, there is merit in reflecting on what they taught you and in what way they might motivate you to change the world. Again, perhaps the client who experienced abuse doesn't want to work for a shelter for abused victims, but that dark moment could fuel her to empower people in whatever career she chooses.

In fact, the low points often contain even more power for preparation than the high ones.

Echoes of Your Strengths and Refinement of Compassion

In summary, the moments when you felt most alive, fulfilled, connected, or joyful are not accidents.

They are echoes—reminders of the strengths and spiritual gifts God placed within you.

When you look at your high points, ask yourself: What gifts was I using during this time? What needs was I helping to meet? What impact did I have on others?

Your strengths often show up most clearly when you're serving selflessly and creating something meaningful.

The valleys of your life—the losses, betrayals, failures, heartbreaks—were not sent by God to destroy you.

They were allowed to refine you.

In the depths of sorrow, we gain:

Deeper empathy

Greater patience

Stronger resilience

Sharper spiritual sensitivity

These qualities are essential for fulfilling a Christ-centered mission.

Think again about Alma the Younger. He wasn't just a rebellious teenager who turned things around. He was actively working against the Church, using his charisma and intellect to tear down faith and lead others into doubt. This wasn't casual wandering—it was intentional destruction (see Mosiah 27:8–10). But God saw past the rebellion to the potential. Alma's divine disruption—that powerful angelic encounter followed by days of soul-wrenching darkness—didn't just rescue him; it refined him. His repentance gave him empathy, his past gave him power, and his pain became the platform for his purpose. Because he had once been blind, he could now help others see. Because he had once fought truth, he could now defend it. His ministry wasn't abstract or theoretical; it was deeply personal. And that's what made it effective. He spoke from scars, not just sermons. And those scars gave him access to hearts that a "polished" or perfect prophet never could have reached.

Your pain equips you to become an instrument of healing in ways you couldn't have imagined otherwise.

The Book of Mormon teaches, "For it must needs be, that there is an opposition in all things" (2 Nephi 2:11)

Opposition isn't evidence that you've been abandoned. It's evidence that you are becoming. Every hero's journey—from Nephi to Esther to Peter to Joseph Smith—involved massive adversity. Their callings didn't spare them from opposition. Their callings required it.

Your story will be no different.

The moments you thought would break you are the very moments that build the muscles you need to carry out your purpose.

How to Read the Clues on Your Journey Map

So you've mapped your journey through life and you're reflecting on the peaks and valleys. You still may feel that you haven't clarified your purpose. In that case, here are three additional sets of questions to guide you.

1. What Themes Keep Emerging?

Look for repeated experiences, feelings, or desires across different seasons of your life.

For example:

- A pattern of defending the underdog
- A recurring love of teaching and explaining
- A habit of creating beauty from chaos
- A constant draw toward healing broken things

These themes aren't coincidences. They're bread crumbs leading you home to your purpose.

2. Where Was God Especially Near?

Identify the moments when you felt God's hand most clearly.

These often include:

- Unexpected peace during a crisis
- Miraculous opportunities
- Lessons learned the hard way
- Comfort that felt larger than your own understanding

Mark these points boldly on your Journey Map. They are signposts—reminders that your life is not random or abandoned.

3. What Burdens Became Blessings?

Sometimes our greatest heartbreaks end up becoming the source of our greatest blessings—not by erasing the pain but by transforming it into power.

Ask yourself:

- What wounds have made me more compassionate?
- What failures taught me humility and resilience?
- What losses helped me value what matters most?

Your burdens may have become blessings in disguise, preparing you for a mission bigger than you dared dream.

Crafting Your Purpose Discovery Statement

Now that you've mapped your highs and lows, studied the patterns, and prayed over the lessons, it's time to capture what you're learning.

Not in a permanent, final way. But in a living, breathing, flexible way.

Introducing the Purpose Discovery Statement.

This is not your final "mission statement" yet—we'll refine that later. This is a first articulation—a faithful draft—of what your Journey Map is revealing about your divine purpose.

How to Create Your Purpose Discovery Statement

Step 1: List Your Core Themes

From your Journey Map, list out the themes you noticed. For example, compassion for the lonely, passion for teaching, desire to build community, hunger for healing, and so on.

Step 2: Identify Your Driving Emotions

Ask:

- What emotions drive me most powerfully?
- What injustice or need stirs righteous anger or profound compassion?
- What experiences make me feel fully alive, fully human?

Step 3: Choose a Verb and a Focus

Good purpose statements start with an action verb. Damon's research shows that purpose isn't just about personal achievement; it always includes an intention to contribute to something beyond the self. That's what separates a self-centered ambition from a God-honoring purpose: One serves only you; the other serves others.

Examples of action verbs include inspire, empower, heal, build, teach, lift, connect, and create.

Then identify a focus. For example: Inspire hope in struggling youth. Heal emotional wounds through storytelling. Build confidence in women leaders. Teach families to strengthen spiritual resilience.

Step 4: Draft a First Attempt

Use this frame: "I am called to [VERB] [FOCUS] through [METHOD]." Or "I exist to [VERB] [FOCUS] through [METHOD]."

For example, "I am called to empower overlooked teenagers through mentorship and storytelling." Or "I exist to heal hearts burdened by grief through teaching truth and creating safe spaces."

Step 5: Pray Over It

Write a few versions. Sit with them. Ask Heavenly Father, "Is this the work Thou hast prepared me for? Am I seeing myself as Thou seest me?"

How will you know when you've nailed it? You should *feel* it. In fact, every time I lead a workshop on clarifying purpose, I always end it by asking a few participants to share their statements without any context or background. They'll proudly proclaim their purpose, and people usually clap. Once they've shared, I'll ask how it *felt* to share. They'll often say things like empowering, honest, vulnerable, powerful, or nervous. And why would it feel that way? Because you're sharing something close to your soul—to your identity—that's raw, powerful, and personal. It's rooted in who you are. You *should* feel it.

So you'll know when you hit upon a statement that feels like home.

It won't necessarily be dramatic. More often, it will feel like a warm, steady, quiet *yes* deep in your spirit.

Purpose Is a Partnership, Not a Project

Important reminder:

You are not creating your purpose alone.

God is your partner in this work.

He sees you clearly. He knows the end from the beginning. He delights in revealing your mission as you seek it with humility, courage, and faith. You don't have to have all the answers yet. You just have to be willing to listen, to learn, and to follow where He leads.

The psalmist wrote, "The steps of a good man are ordered by the Lord: and he delighteth in his way." (Psalm 37:23)

Trust that God is ordering your steps—even now.

Final Reflection: The Beauty of Your Becoming

If you leave this chapter with only one truth burned into your soul, let it be this:

You are not behind. You are not broken. You are becoming.

Every high, every low, every twist and turn of your story has been preparing you—patiently, lovingly—for the work you were born to do. Your Journey Map is not a record of random events. It is the sacred curriculum of your becoming.

And as you walk forward with faith, more and more of your divine purpose will come into view—shining clearer and brighter, just like the morning sun. You were sent here for a reason. You were sent here for now. You were sent here for them.

Let's continue uncovering the masterpiece God is creating through you.

4

Crafting Your Purpose Statement

"Efforts and courage are not enough without purpose and direction."—John F. Kennedy[31]

"We are not here in this life to waste time. We are here to gain experience and to become better than we were." —President Thomas S. Monson

---

By now, you've taken a long, courageous look back at your life through the Journey Map.

You've seen the highs, the lows, the lessons, and the fingerprints of God in places you once thought were barren.

You've started sensing the themes and the callings that have been quietly rising to the surface of your story.

Now it's time to do something bold.

It's time to name your purpose.

Not perfectly. Not permanently. But powerfully.

Because when you put words to your calling, it shifts from a fuzzy idea to a focused intention—something you can live by, pray over, and build your life around.

In this chapter, you'll learn how to create a purpose statement that captures the unique mission God has placed within you.

Why You Need a Purpose Statement

Words have power.

They clarify, focus, and motivate.

When you can clearly articulate your purpose, it becomes a compass for your decisions, relationships, priorities, and dreams. Without a purpose statement, it's easy to drift through life reacting to whatever shows up. With a purpose statement, you live by design—not by default.

Gallup's 2023 global workplace study found that only 23 percent of employees worldwide are actively engaged in their work.[32] One of the biggest drivers of disengagement? A lack of personal purpose. People don't just want a paycheck—they want to know their hours are adding up to something. When you don't have a sense of why you're doing what you do, even success starts to feel hollow.

Think of your purpose statement as:

- A guiding North Star
- A battle cry when things get hard
- A measuring stick for what deserves your yes (and what deserves your no)

Clarity creates courage.

When you know why you're here, you stop wasting energy on what doesn't matter—and you start pouring your strength into what matters most.

What a Great Purpose Statement Looks Like

A strong purpose statement has three key qualities.

1. It's Clear

No jargon.

No buzzwords.

No ten-dollar words that confuse more than they inspire.

It should be so simple and clear that a teenager could understand it immediately.

Example: "To heal broken hearts through honest storytelling."

2. It's Short

Again, brevity is key for memory. Aim for ten words or fewer. Long, complicated purpose statements end up in desk drawers. Short, powerful ones end up in your daily prayers and decisions.

Examples:

- "To ignite courage in young leaders."
- "To build belonging for those who feel unseen."
- "To awaken hope through teaching and mentorship."

3. It's Action-Oriented

Your purpose isn't passive. It's active.

It starts with a verb:

- Inspire
- Create
- Heal
- Empower
- Connect
- Defend
- Teach
- Build
- Lead

You are called to *do* something in the world—not just to *be* something.

How to Write Your Purpose Statement

Here's the simple, step-by-step process:

Step 1: Review Your Journey Map

Look back at the high points and low points you mapped earlier and the draft statement you began to craft.

Ask:

- What threads or themes keep appearing?
- What gifts or passions show up repeatedly?
- What burdens or causes stir my heart most deeply?

Step 2: Identify Your Core Contribution

Your purpose isn't about making yourself famous. It's about contributing to others.

Ask:

- Who am I most drawn to serve?
- What need or problem am I uniquely positioned to address?
- Where does my joy meet the world's deep hunger?

Step 3: Choose Your Power Verb

Pick a verb that captures your action. For example:

- Inspire
- Empower
- Heal
- Uplift
- Build
- Guide
- Advocate
- Create
- Awaken
- Teach
- Transform

Your verb should feel energetic and alive—something you can imagine doing with passion.

Step 4: Define Your Audience or Focus

Who or what will you impact?
Be as specific as you can without being restrictive.
Examples:

- Young leaders
- Broken families
- Women in transition
- Overlooked communities
- People seeking healing
- Families of faith

Step 5: Draft a One-Sentence Statement

Use this basic frame: "I am called to [VERB] [AUDIENCE] by [METHOD/FOCUS]."

Examples:

- "I am called to empower young adults to believe in their potential."
- "I am called to heal broken marriages through Christ-centered counseling."
- "I am called to awaken creativity in weary souls through storytelling and art."

Write several versions. Play with the wording. Don't stress about getting it perfect. Listen for the one that makes your spirit leap a little.

That's the one.

Common Mistakes When Writing Your Purpose Statement

Mistake 1: Making It Too Complicated

Don't try to cram everything into one bloated sentence. A great purpose statement is simple and focused.

I've generally found that the shorter the purpose statement, the more powerful it becomes. In other words, your purpose isn't a paragraph or a story but a statement—a rallying cry. It's a motto that's easy to recall and that holds some meaning for you in your work.

Mistake 2: Focusing Too Much on Yourself

Purpose is not about making your life easier—it's about lifting others. True purpose always points outward.

I once got an email from a medical student who attended my seminar on finding core purpose in work. He reflected on what I had shared for several weeks and decided that he helps people to prove that "he's worth it" to justify his existence on the planet. In short, he said his purpose is to "give myself value." He asked if this felt like an unhealthy mindset because it was self-focused.

I replied, "First off, great job reflecting on your purpose. You're more likely to be intentional by doing so. Well done. Second, I'm hesitant to provide 'feedback' on someone's life purpose, because only you will know when you've hit it, and everyone's is different.

"That said, I would press you on these three words. I've found that core purpose is generally outward-directed, meaning to the benefit of humankind. Remember the examples: improving customer experience, maximizing human potential, etc. It sounds like proving your worth may be a value (affirmation?) but is perhaps not a core purpose. I'd go a step further with it and ask 'why' you like to help people, 'what' people, and 'to what end.'"

In other words, if your purpose feels self-serving, you may not be there yet. A life purpose is most often outward-facing, since serving the greater good seems to be a key driver for most of us.

Mistake 3: Waiting for Absolute Certainty Before Writing

Too many people stall out because they think purpose should arrive fully formed—like one perfect sentence written in stone. But clarity doesn't usually come that way. More often, it comes through movement. You don't need a burning bush. You need a willingness to begin.

Start with your best thinking. Write what feels most true right now, even if it's not perfect. You can revise. You can evolve. Purpose tends to reveal itself more clearly in motion than in stillness. Waiting for 100 percent certainty before you act usually means you'll never start.

God works with the willing, not the perfect.

Refining Your Statement: The Test of Resonance

Ask yourself:

- Does this make me feel energized?
- Does it feel like a reflection of who I'm becoming?
- Can I imagine waking up each day excited to live this out?

If yes, you're on track. If not, revise it. Purpose should spark something inside you—a quiet thrill, a swelling courage, a hopeful YES.

Another homework assignment I give my workshop participants: Once you've crafted your statement, I want you to go and share it out loud with at least three other people. Tell them you've been in a workshop on purpose and that you developed a statement and want to share it. Then share it.

But here's the key: You are *not* seeking feedback. They'll undoubtedly give it to you anyway, but I don't really care what they have to say. This isn't about them. The goal of sharing it is two-fold:

1. When you say it out loud, you'll naturally edit it. You'll change words and say it more succinctly. Pay attention to your self-edits.
1. Note how you *feel* when you say it out loud. Does it pump you up? Do you feel powerful?

If it feels unemotional or soulless, you're not there yet. So go back and edit it and work on it some more. Refine it until you feel it.

Spiritual Confirmation: Partnering with God

Your purpose is sacred. It's not just a personal project—it's a divine collaboration. So take some time to review the statement with the God who planted it in you in the first place. You've done the hard work of studying it out; now seek confirmation.

Step 1: Pray

"Heavenly Father, is this the work Thou hast prepared for me? Is this how Thou would have me serve?"

Step 2: Seek Patterns

Pay attention to repeated impressions, scriptures, or messages that confirm or refine your direction. I oftentimes tell people that the Holy Ghost manifests in your search for purpose as "repeating patterns of thought during unintuitive moments consistently over time." Let's break that down.

"Repeating patterns" means that you have the same thought over and over again. "During unintuitive moments" means that these patterns of thought come when you're not proactively or intentionally thinking about it. Think: showering, mowing the lawn, commuting, or resting. You're not sitting down with pen and paper to figure it out, but the whisper comes when you least expect it, and you catch the thought before it flees.

"Consistently over time" means the thought doesn't just come to you once or twice—it comes today, tomorrow, next week, a month later, and maybe for years. In fact, I've learned that the thought won't stop coming until I do something about it. In addition, I'm afraid of the day that the thought does stop coming because I didn't do anything about it and the Lord gave it to someone else to do!

Step 3: Be Open to Adjustment

God may lead you to sharpen, simplify, or expand your statement over time. Don't be too enamored with your statement. The great Editor has insight about us that we may never have.

Declaring Your Purpose Out Loud

Once you feel aligned with your purpose statement, say it.

Out loud.

Often.

"I am called to ____________." Or "I exist to ___________."

Say it in the mirror, in prayer, and to trusted friends or mentors. Write it on sticky notes. Make it your phone wallpaper.

Own it.

What to Expect After Declaring Your Purpose

I've found that people who share their purpose notice some interesting things begin to happen.

1. Opportunities Will Start Showing Up

This isn't magic. It's focus.

Before you clarified your purpose, the world was just noise. You were living in reaction—bouncing between obligations, distractions, and whatever felt urgent.

But once you name your purpose, something shifts. Your awareness sharpens. Your mind starts filtering for alignment. Suddenly, things you used to scroll past or ignore—conversations, doors, resources, nudges—start standing out.

Why? Because your brain is wired to notice whatever you've told it is important. It's the same reason you suddenly see your new car everywhere after buying it. Your purpose has become your lens—and now you're seeing through it. Research in cognitive psychology calls this the *priming effect*—once your mind is "primed" with a goal, you unconsciously start noticing related opportunities. For example, those who have recently bought a new car begin seeing that model everywhere. In the same way, naming your purpose mentally primes you to recognize opportunities you might have previously overlooked.

What's at the root?

Clarity creates direction. And direction activates spiritual momentum. God has likely been sending opportunities your way all along—but now you're finally awake enough to notice and brave enough to respond.

Think of someone starting a small community service initiative. At first, they struggle—with finding participants, resources, or momentum. But with a clear purpose—such as "I exist to uplift underserved families"—they begin to notice volunteer leads, opportunities for grants, and unexpected collaborations. Their work takes shape not because they planned it perfectly but because their purpose primed them to see openings and persist when others would abandon ship.

2. Opposition Will Increase

This one catches people off guard. They assume that once they've found their purpose, life should get easier. The clouds part, the sun shines, the angels start handing out job offers.

But that's not what happens.

What happens is resistance.

Old insecurities flare up. Unexpected criticism shows up. Doubts start whispering louder than before. You hit walls—relationally, emotionally, spiritually.

Why?

Because stepping into your divine identity puts pressure on everything that's not aligned with it. It shakes up the status quo—internally and externally.

What's at the root?

You've entered spiritual territory now. And the enemy doesn't need to attack people who are asleep at the wheel—he goes after the ones who are waking up. Resistance is not a sign that you've done something wrong. It's often proof that you're on sacred ground.

And here's the paradox: That resistance will refine you. Just like heat strengthens steel, opposition strengthens resolve. It matures your mission. It burns away ego and forces you to depend on grace.

So don't resent the resistance. Learn from it. Let it build you.

3. Purpose Will Continue to Evolve

Some people get nervous once they write their purpose statement. They think it has to be perfect. Final. Set in stone.

But purpose doesn't work that way. It's not a formula—it's a relationship.

As you grow, your understanding of your calling will grow with you. As your heart heals, your influence will widen. As your faith deepens, your voice will shift. God will show you new layers, new directions, new assignments.

What's at the root?

Purpose isn't a one-time revelation. It's an ongoing invitation. The more you walk with God, the more He reveals.

You don't have to be afraid of this evolution. It doesn't mean you were wrong before—it means you're maturing. Think of it like a tree: Your purpose is rooted in the same soil, but the branches are stretching wider, higher, fuller with time.

So hold your purpose statement with open hands. It's not a static label. It's a living, breathing reflection of who you're becoming in Christ.

Final Reflection: You Are Needed

Maybe you still feel nervous. Maybe part of you wonders, "Who am I to claim a purpose this bold? Why would God trust someone like me with a sacred work?"

You are exactly the kind of person God delights in using. Not because you're flawless but because you're faithful. You have been placed here, in this time, with your particular gifts and experiences, for a reason.

President Dieter F. Uchtdorf said, "The Lord knows you. He knows your heart and is pleased with your sacrifice. He smiles upon you each day. He will uphold you and prepare the way for you. He will send His angels before you. You will feel their presence. And with the help of heaven, your talents will be multiplied. I promise you that as you lift those around you, the Lord God, the Creator of the universe, will lift you up. If you will only believe and incline your heart to our Beloved Father, He will place within you a peace that surpasses understanding. He will give you joy. May each of you always remember this."[33] Your placement is not random. God factored in your strengths, your struggles, your timing, and your temperament. You were sent on purpose—with purpose.

You are needed. Your light is needed. Your voice is needed. Your faith is needed.

The Lord is counting on you—not to be perfect but to be present.

And you are ready.

5

The Villains of Purpose: Overcoming What Holds You Back

"Satan trembles when he sees the weakest saint upon their knees." —William Cowper[34]

You've mapped your journey. You've discovered the gifts hiding in your valleys. You've even started shaping your purpose statement—something bold, sacred, and aligned with God's will for you.

But right around now, something happens for most people.

The inner war begins.

Just as you begin stepping into your divine identity, you start hearing voices. Doubts. Delays. Distractions. Resistance.

These are the villains of purpose.

They are the silent killers that convince too many people to shrink, to stall, or to silently quit before they've even really begun.

Every great story has a villain. Every divine mission has opposition.

Your purpose does too.

That doesn't mean you're doing something wrong. In fact, it often means you're getting really close to something holy.

Annie's Resistance

Annie had always been someone who felt deeply connected to helping others, a value she inherited from her mother. As a young adult, she followed this path by enrolling in nursing school, believing that a career in healthcare would allow her to care for others in meaningful ways. However, during her time in nursing, something felt off. Despite the alignment between her values and the work she was doing, Annie experienced a growing sense of dissatisfaction and unease. Nursing wasn't giving her the fulfillment she had expected, and she struggled to admit that she didn't enjoy the work.

The turning point came when Annie made the courageous decision to leave nursing. It was difficult—she had invested so much time and energy into the profession, and it felt like admitting defeat. Yet once she allowed herself to stop, she felt a sense of freedom that she hadn't felt in a long time. Still, this newfound freedom came with its own challenges—Annie felt stuck and unsure of what her next steps should be. She faced a period of feeling lost and lacking direction, and she even turned to prescription medication to cope with the emotional strain.

Through this difficult time, Annie began a process of self-reflection. She asked herself hard questions about what truly mattered to her, what brought her joy, and what kind of impact she wanted to have in the world. She realized that while nursing wasn't the right fit, her desire to help others, particularly those who couldn't help themselves, remained a core part of her identity.

This realization was reinforced by her love for animals and her natural instinct to care for them. Annie reflected on how she always surrounded herself with pets, making sure they felt loved and understood. She connected this nurturing side of herself to a broader purpose: helping those—whether people or animals—who couldn't help themselves.

Looking back at her life's highs and lows, Annie saw a consistent theme: She felt fulfilled when she was supporting others, particularly in moments where they lacked the means to do it themselves. Whether it was during her time in nursing or taking care of her pets, Annie's heart was most alive when she was in service to the vulnerable. Even in her toughest moments, like overcoming her reliance on prescription medication, Annie's motivation to help others never wavered—it was, in fact, her lowest point that pushed her to seek deeper clarity about her purpose.

Annie ultimately defined her purpose in one clear, moving statement: "I exist to help those who cannot help themselves." With this newfound clarity, she was able to reframe her next steps in life. She realized that her career didn't have to follow a traditional path—it simply needed to allow her to live out her purpose of helping others in the way that felt most true to her heart.

Annie's story serves as a reminder that purpose is almost always accompanied by resistance—mostly in the form of internal villains. Sometimes it takes leaving behind what doesn't serve us, facing difficult lows, and reflecting on what truly makes us feel alive. For Annie, discovering her purpose didn't just help her plot a new career path—it helped her find a deeper sense of direction in life, rooted in service and compassion.

You've just entered the battlefield. You will undoubtedly feel resistance as you embark on the journey of aligning your life with your purpose, but with knowledge of the enemy comes confidence that you can win.

And now it's time to learn how to fight.

Villain #1: Doubt and Fear

Fear is usually the first villain to show up.

When Carly got called to be the Relief Society president, she smiled and said yes—and then went home and cried in her car.

She wasn't doubting the Lord. She was doubting herself. She felt too young, too emotionally raw, and too underqualified to step into a calling that had once been held by women twice her age with decades of experience. The voice started early: "Who do you think you are? They're going to see right through you. You're not spiritually strong enough for this."

For the first few weeks, she didn't wrestle with logistics. She wrestled with shame. Every meeting felt like a test she wasn't passing. Every sister's trial felt like more than she could hold. But slowly, something shifted. Not because the calling got easier, but because Carly stopped showing up to prove herself and started showing up to serve.

The voice didn't go away overnight. But it lost power. Because her obedience got louder than her insecurity.

She was learning what most people living their purpose eventually discover: The enemy won't usually try to stop your calling—he'll just try to convince you you're unworthy of it.

Right after someone dares to name their purpose, the fear-based thoughts come rushing in.

"Who do you think you are?"

"You're not good enough."

"You're too late."

"You're not spiritual enough."

"You'll mess this up."

Fear loves to attack identity. If it can get you to doubt your worth, you'll never act on your purpose.

But fear is not from God. "For God hath not given us the spirit of fear; but of power, and of love, and of a sound mind" (2 Timothy 1:7).

Fear will always be part of the journey. But it doesn't get to drive.

I've coached thousands of people through career changes, faith transitions, leadership roles, and big life leaps. Every single one of them heard the voice of fear. Every one.

But the difference between those who move forward and those who stay stuck?

The ones who move forward learned to act in spite of fear—not wait until it disappeared. It almost never goes away! I once heard a leadership guru say that there are two kinds of fear: First, there's the kind that prevents you from physical harm and pain, like putting your hand on a stove or running in front of a car. That's good fear, and you should listen to it because it will keep you alive. But the second kind of fear is the kind that stops us from doing what we should be doing, and that's the fear of failure. When that fear comes, acknowledge it, even tip your hat to it, then say, "Thanks for the heads up . . . I'm going to do this anyway." Then punch it in the face and move forward.

Faith isn't the absence of fear. Faith is choosing to believe that God's promises are bigger than your insecurities.

Villain #2: Comparison

When I was a teenager, my mom used to leave little notes on my mirror to inspire me. It was her way of reaching me at a time when I was otherwise a bit stubborn, uninterested in advice, or simply focused on other things. I don't remember any of the notes she left except one: "The greatest unhappiness you will experience in your life comes from comparing yourself to others."

Comparison is a shape-shifter. It's sneaky. It creeps in quietly, usually through the side door of your phone.

You scroll through someone's Instagram post about their thriving business, perfect family, or latest mission trip and suddenly your purpose—which felt so exciting an hour ago—now feels small and stupid.

"Why even try? Someone else is already doing it—better."

Here's the truth: Someone out there is smarter, faster, better-funded, more photogenic, and has way more followers than you. Cool. Good for them.

But that doesn't cancel your calling.

Your purpose is not a competition. It's a covenant.

The people you're called to reach will not respond to anyone else the way they will respond to you—your voice, your story, your specific mix of pain and perspective and power.

God didn't make a mistake when He assigned your purpose to you. He didn't run out of better people. He chose you on purpose, for a purpose.

Get out of everyone else's lane. Own your own race.

Villain #3: Distraction

Distraction doesn't feel evil. It feels busy.

It shows up as a to-do list that never ends, a hundred open browser tabs, another Netflix binge, and hours of numbing your brain with TikTok or scrolling Zillow listings for homes you'll never buy.

Distraction is dangerous because it doesn't feel like rebellion—but it robs you just the same.

In April 2001, Elder Richard G. Scott said, "Satan has a powerful tool to use against good people. It is distraction. He would have good people fill life with 'good things' so there is no room for the essential ones."[35]

Distraction kills your clarity. It crowds out revelation. It drowns the still, small voice.

If Satan can't make you disobedient, he'll try to make you distracted.

One of the adversary's favorite tools is to keep you so overwhelmed with the urgent that you forget the important.

Distraction doesn't have to look evil to be effective. Sometimes it looks like comfort. Or busyness. Or goals that look good on the outside but have nothing to do with your calling. And when you forget why you were sent here, it's easy to trade the eternal for the urgent.

Elder Marvin J. Ashton illustrated this with a powerfully sobering metaphor:

> What young musician, finally scheduled to debut in a capacity concert hall after years of agonizing rehearsal, would, while en route to the performance, stop to join a long line forming at the latest hit movie, forgetting the thousands of people waiting to hear her?
>
> What world-class runner, after training for well over a decade, would find himself in the Olympic finals, only to stop running halfway through his race to watch the high-jump finals taking place on the other side of the field?
>
> These examples may seem preposterous—but how much more tragic it is for someone who, equipped with a testimony of the truth and a knowledge of the purpose of life, becomes more absorbed in life today than in life forever. . . . I fear that, at times, we run the risk of acting like seasoned, conditioned athletes who are more interested in what kind of jogging suits we'll wear than in buckling down to train for the race.[36]

What's the solution?

Simplicity. Sabbath. Stillness.

Start setting boundaries. Put your phone down. Make white space in your calendar for God to speak.

Create intentional rhythms of silence and solitude—even five minutes a day—where you reconnect to your purpose and tune in to His voice.

Villain #4: Perfectionism

Perfectionism says, "If I can't do this flawlessly, I won't do it at all."

This villain often disguises itself as excellence or spiritual worthiness. But it's a liar.

Perfectionism paralyzes you. It tricks you into believing that your value is based on your performance, that your worth depends on getting everything right the first time.

But the gospel doesn't teach performance-based love. It teaches grace-based progress. This is a vital distinction—and one that many wrestle with, often unknowingly. In a culture that prizes achievement, efficiency, and visible success, it's easy to carry those values into our spiritual life. We start believing, perhaps subtly, that God is most pleased when we're impressive. That His love increases when our scripture study is consistent, our callings are executed flawlessly, or our family looks picture-perfect at church.

But that's not the gospel. That's a distortion of it.

God's love is not a reward for good behavior. It is the eternal starting point. God's love is infinite and will endure forever. It is not diminished by our mistakes. We cannot earn it any more than we can earn the sunlight.

Grace is not reserved for the finish line. It's the power that gets you through the race. And progress in the gospel is not measured by how quickly you perform but by how deeply you rely.

Grace-based progress acknowledges that growth is messy. That setbacks are part of sanctification. That spiritual transformation takes time, trust, and the willingness to get back up. It's the reason the Savior says, "Come unto me," not "Impress me." His invitation isn't reserved for the polished and prepared—it's extended to the weary and willing.

When we internalize this truth, it frees us from the exhausting treadmill of spiritual perfectionism. We stop performing for approval and start walking with purpose. We stop fearing failure and start trusting grace. We begin to understand that the gospel is not a report card—it's a relationship. And that relationship is grounded not in our ability to check all the boxes but in Christ's power to change our hearts.

God doesn't need you to get it perfect. He needs you to show up with a willing heart.

Let me tell you a secret I've learned while coaching high achievers: Most of them secretly feel like frauds. They're terrified someone will find out they're making it up as they go. I remember when I launched Proof Leadership Group, and we began coaching executives. I too felt some impostor syndrome. "What can I possibly add to these high-achievers' journey?" But I learned very quickly that they are humans who are gifted at a few things but feel the same impostor syndrome we all feel in many other ways.

Welcome to the club. The purpose path is messy.

There's no such thing as a flawless disciple. There's only one perfect being in this story, and it's not you.

The rest of us get to walk with a limp.

Villain #5: Failure

Let's talk about failure. Not the kind you shrug off or laugh about later. I mean real, hard, gut-punching, ego-shattering failure. The kind that makes you question everything—your calling, your worth, even your sanity.

Most people assume that failure means they're off track. That they must have misheard God, made the wrong move, or taken a leap they weren't qualified for. But more often than not, failure doesn't mean you're lost. It means you're finally walking into territory big enough to matter. You're stepping outside the safety of the known and putting your faith into motion.

Failure is not the opposite of purpose. It's part of the path.

I think about Carrie, a client of mine with a fire in her heart to launch a ministry for women who had left the Church but were aching to reconnect with God. She poured everything into it—her savings, her late nights, her soul—and then it bombed. Year one ended in heartbreak. Her events didn't fill. Her team fell apart. The response was tepid. She slipped into silence, convinced she had misunderstood her prompting.

But in the dark? God wasn't done.

He used that year to reshape her from the inside out. He stripped away her need for validation and reoriented her focus from performance to presence. Year two looked nothing like the launch plan. It was smaller. Quieter. But also more grounded. She stopped trying to impress and started trying to obey. And slowly, the doors opened. Not all at once. But enough to show her that the failure wasn't the end. It was the forge.

Because that's what failure does. It refines you. It humbles your ego and sharpens your empathy. It purifies your motives. It deepens the authority of your voice, not because you nailed it but because you survived it.

Scripture is packed with people who failed hard before they flourished. Moses ran away. Peter denied. Alma the Younger fought the very church he later led. Their failures didn't disqualify them. They prepared them.

So if you're sitting in the ashes of a dream that didn't work, don't assume you missed your purpose. This might be where your purpose is finally being made real. Let Him use the failure to shape the fire. He's not done. And neither are you.

Villain #6: Shame

Shame is fear's uglier cousin.

Where fear says, "You might fail," shame says, "You *are* a failure."

In the April 2025 general conference, Sister Tamara Runia made two powerful statements on shame that have rattled in my head since: "Shame is a darkness so heavy it feels that if you took it out of your body, it would have an actual weight or heft to it." And "shame doesn't tell us we made a mistake; it tells us we are our mistakes."[37]

Shame doesn't attack your actions—it attacks your identity.

When Marco was called into the elders quorum presidency, his first thought wasn't "What an honor." It was "This is a mistake."

He'd only been active again for a couple of years after stepping away from the Church in college. He still felt a little out of place on

Sundays—like someone might eventually tap him on the shoulder and say, "Hey, we meant the other guy." He worried he didn't know the handbook well enough, didn't have the right tone, didn't look the part.

But more than that, he carried this weight that he had too much past and not enough polish to be leading anyone spiritually.

In his first few meetings, he second-guessed everything. He waited for someone to challenge his credibility. No one did. They asked for help, and he helped. They needed someone to listen, and he showed up.

Somewhere in the middle of making visits and organizing moves and sitting in on priesthood interviews, Marco realized something: His past wasn't disqualifying him—it was equipping him. The empathy he thought disqualified him was actually the bridge.

And the villain he'd been fighting? It wasn't judgment from others. It was the lie that God only calls people with clean résumés and spotless records.

Shame tells you:

- "You'll never be enough."
- "If people knew the real you, they'd walk away."
- "You're damaged goods."
- "God might love you in theory, but He can't really use you."

Let me tell you something clearly: That is not God's voice.

Jesus came to silence shame.

He didn't just come to save you from sin—He came to restore you to your calling.

Romans 8:1 declares, "There is therefore now no condemnation to them which are in Christ Jesus."

Chary's Resilience

Chary's story is one of my favorites because she experienced failure and shame and fought through it. Chary's path toward discovering her purpose was shaped by a series of personal highs and lows, each of which brought her closer to understanding what truly mattered to her. Throughout her life, she faced challenges that tested her resolve and reshaped her perspective on what it meant to live with purpose.

One of the pivotal moments in Chary's life was when she left a PsyD program that she had worked so hard to enter. Leaving the program felt like failure, but it was a turning point. The decision to step away came after years of health struggles and personal challenges that forced her to reevaluate what was truly important. In hindsight, this moment of "failure" wasn't about giving up but about gaining clarity. It taught Chary that it was okay to change course when something wasn't right and that success isn't defined by pushing through at all costs—it's about finding the path that aligns with who you truly are.

Chary's journey was also shaped by her work as a behavioral aide for children, where she discovered a deep passion for helping kids learn and grow. While working with a young boy who had difficulties with verbal communication, Chary realized that music was a key that unlocked his ability to express himself. This experience sparked her interest in child development and showed her that she had a natural gift for helping children connect with the world around them. This moment of discovery became a foundational part of her journey, guiding her into a career where she could merge her intellectual interests with her passion for helping children.

As she reflected on her life, Chary realized that the moments that brought her the most fulfillment were those where she had been able to help children play, explore, and learn. These moments stood in stark contrast to the times when she felt lost or disconnected—especially in environments where she didn't feel supported or understood. Reflecting on these highs and lows, Chary's purpose became clear: She existed to create a world where children could explore, play, and learn without fear of failure, in environments that supported their growth and imagination.

Her purpose statement, "I exist to make the world a playful and imaginative space for kids," became a guiding light for her future decisions. It reminded her that her struggles had shaped her into someone uniquely qualified to create spaces where children could thrive, and it gave her a renewed sense of direction as she moved forward in her career.

She came to coaching convinced her past was too dark to share. But when she finally opened up, something broke. God met her in the wreckage. And she realized her pain wasn't proof she was disqualified. It was the soil for her purpose.

Now she helps women reclaim their stories. What shame tried to silence, God is now using as a microphone.

President Jeffrey R. Holland has said, "Don't you quit. You keep walking. You keep trying. There is help and happiness ahead—a lot of it."[38] When we look back at the trials we've faced, it's often in hindsight that we see God's hand guiding us through them. These experiences can reveal not only how much we've grown but also what unique strengths we've gained that may be central to our purpose.

Spiritual Opposition: The Enemy of Purpose

Living your purpose will invite resistance. Not just from your schedule, your finances, or your own doubts—but from the adversary himself.

This is spiritual warfare.

We don't talk about it enough, especially when we're helping people uncover their divine identity. But we should. Because the moment you start living with intention—the moment you begin to align your life with God's mission—you become a threat to the kingdom of darkness.

Satan knows what happens when sons and daughters of God wake up to who they really are. When you start walking in your purpose, you stop settling. You stop hiding. You stop numbing out. You start building, healing, loving, teaching, creating—and every bit of that pushes back darkness. You are more proactive and intentional every day, and you live your life on purpose.

So the opposition comes.

Not always with a pitchfork and horns. Sometimes it's just a heavy fog of discouragement. A sudden wave of shame. A perfectly timed distraction. A subtle whisper: "Who do you think you are to do this?"

The enemy doesn't care what it takes—insecurity, exhaustion, temptation, fear—as long as it slows you down, silences your voice, or stops your forward movement. The enemy doesn't have to steal your gifts. He just has to convince you never to use them.

As the writer Sydney Smith said, "A great deal of talent is lost to the world for the want of a little courage. Every day sends to their graves . . . [those] who have only remained obscure because their timidity has prevented them from making a first effort."[39]

But here's the good news: You weren't built to back down.

You've been given the armor of God for a reason. You've been equipped, commissioned, and covered. You don't fight alone, and you don't fight empty-handed. You fight with the Word. With the Spirit. With truth. With grace. With community. With the authority of someone who knows exactly who they are in Christ.

So the next time the voice of the enemy creeps in, asking, "Who do you think you are?"—you answer without blinking:

"I'm a child of God. I'm called. I'm covered. I'm chosen. And I'm not quitting."

How to Push Back: Practical Weapons

Spiritual warfare might be invisible, but that doesn't mean you're defenseless. Here are some weapons you can use in real time when the battle hits close.

Name the Voice

When fear or shame shows up, call it out. Say it out loud if you have to: "That's not God's voice." There is power in naming the lie. The enemy thrives in secrecy—but truth breaks his hold.

Return to Your Purpose

When you feel lost, overwhelmed, or unsure, go back to what you know. Read your purpose statement. Pray over it. Speak it out loud. Remind yourself why you started. Remind yourself who called you.

Take One Brave Step

Don't wait to feel ready. Courage doesn't always feel like a roar—sometimes it's just clicking "send" on the email, making the phone call, writing the first paragraph. Do the next faithful thing, even if your hands are shaking.

Bring It into the Light

Tell someone. Darkness loses power when it's exposed. Whether it's a mentor, a spouse, a bishop, or a trusted friend, let someone know where you're struggling. Don't carry it alone.

Call on Grace

This isn't about powering through in your own strength. You were never meant to white-knuckle your way through purpose. The Atonement of Jesus Christ is not just for your sin—it's for your weakness, your fatigue, and your stuckness. Grace isn't just the rescue rope. It's the fuel.

Final Words: You Are Not the Villain

You are not your fear.
You are not your failure.
You are not your shame.
You are not too late.
You are not too broken.
You are not disqualified.
You are the hero of this story. And heroes keep going.
The world is waiting. Don't let the villains win.
You were born for this.

6

Staying Anchored in Purpose and Personal Revelation

"Knowing that it is in the nature of all things to drift, we must firmly set our anchors on the bedrock of gospel truth. They must not be lightly lowered onto the sands of pride or barely touching the surface of our convictions." —President Dieter F. Uchtdorf[40]

Finding your purpose is powerful.

But staying anchored in it, especially when life hits back—that's where the real growth happens.

See, discovering your purpose is like receiving spiritual coordinates. Living it is like sailing across open, often stormy water. The winds change. The fog rolls in. The shore disappears from view. And suddenly you're not even sure if you're headed the right way anymore.

This is where most people drift.

Not because they're weak. Not because their purpose wasn't real. But because they didn't know how to stay anchored when the waves hit.

Purpose is not a one-time download from heaven. It's a living relationship. It requires maintenance, intimacy, and revelation.

In this chapter, we're going to get super practical and super spiritual—because that's what anchoring takes. We'll talk about how to keep your purpose steady when life is anything but, and how to stay connected to the source: personal revelation.

Why Staying Anchored Matters

Let's be honest: Purpose starts off exciting.

It's like a spiritual adrenaline rush. You've named your mission, you've felt the Spirit confirm it, you've started seeing clues all around you. You shared it with your best friend, significant other, and dog and got positive affirmations from all of them.

But give it a few weeks—or days—and real life sets in.

The bills still have to be paid. Your boss still micromanages. Your kids still throw up on your shoes. That dream project you launched got three likes, and no one responded to the email you worked on for two hours.

Suddenly the question creeps in: Was this really my purpose, or did I just get emotionally hyped?

That's why anchoring matters. Anchoring keeps you steady when emotions fade, grounds you in truth when circumstances lie, and keeps your purpose from becoming another abandoned New Year's resolution.

Jesus told a story about this—the parable of the wise and foolish builders.

One built on sand. The other on rock. The storms came for both. The difference wasn't in the weather—it was in the foundation.

You want to live your purpose long term? Build it on rock. That's what anchoring is.

How People Drift from Their Purpose

Let's name a few common ways people drift.

- They forget the "why." Purpose becomes just another to-do list, not a holy calling.

- They expect immediate results. When purpose doesn't produce fast fruit, they assume it failed.
- They stop seeking revelation. They treat purpose like a one-time event, not an ongoing conversation with God.
- They don't protect their time. Distraction and busyness creep back in and start crowding out intention.
- They confuse resistance with redirection. They hit opposition and think "Maybe I was wrong" instead of "Maybe this matters."

If any of these sound familiar, good. You're not broken—you're normal.

But we're not here to stay stuck. We're here to reset, refocus, and re-anchor.

How to Stay Anchored in Your Purpose

Let's talk about the practices that actually work. This isn't about hype—it's about habits. These are the rhythms and rituals that keep your soul locked into the mission when the grind gets real.

1. Revisit Your Purpose Statement—Daily

Put your purpose statement where you can see it. I'm serious. On your bathroom mirror. In your wallet. Set it as your phone lock screen. Tattoo it on your forehead (okay, maybe not that one). Read it out loud every day. In the mirror. In the car. While folding laundry.

Why?

Because what you rehearse, you remember. And what you remember, you live.

Your purpose needs to be in front of you constantly—because the world is throwing distractions at you hourly.

2. Schedule Purpose Time

If you don't schedule it, it doesn't exist.

Make regular time on your calendar for purpose-driven action. This could look like:

- Blocking thirty minutes each morning for creative work or planning
- Setting a "purpose hour" once a week where you pray, reflect, and review progress
- Committing Sunday nights to purpose journaling and realignment

Your calendar reveals your priorities. Put your purpose on it.

3. Create a Spiritual Routine That Feeds You

If you want to stay anchored, you've got to stay connected to the anchor Himself. This is where personal revelation comes in. You don't need more information—you need illumination.

God is the source of your purpose. And if you want to keep walking in it, you've got to stay in conversation with Him.

Make space for:

- Daily scripture study, especially the Book of Mormon.
- Personal prayer—not just rote repetition, but real, honest, wrestling-with-God kind of prayer.
- Listening. Like actual silence. No music. No noise. Just you, the Spirit, and a notebook.

As you read the scriptures, read them through the lens of your purpose, seeking guidance about how you can better fulfill your mission. You'll be surprised to see the stories of prophets and leaders come to life in a new way and give you insight into how to approach your life's work.

President Russell M. Nelson said, "In coming days, it will not be possible to survive spiritually without the guiding, directing, comforting, and constant influence of the Holy Ghost."[41]

Surviving is one thing. Living your purpose? That takes even more sensitivity.

Ask every day: "God, what would Thou want me to do today that aligns with my purpose?"

Sometimes you'll get specific direction. Sometimes it'll just be peace. Both are sacred.

4. Track Your Purpose Wins

Your brain is hardwired to focus on what's not working. You need to train it to notice what *is*.

Every day or week, jot down:

- Where you lived in alignment with your purpose
- Who you served or impacted (even in tiny ways)
- What gave you life or lit you up

This is like rocket fuel for momentum. You'll start seeing evidence that your purpose is real, active, and fruitful—even if the harvest is small right now.

When the Path Gets Foggy: Staying Tuned In

What about when the spiritual sky gets cloudy?

You were sure of your purpose. You had momentum. Things were clicking.

Then *boom*. Silence. Confusion. Resistance. Or worse, nothing.

No feedback. No fruit. No fire.

These are the wilderness moments. The spiritual fog. And they can feel brutal.

But hear this: The fog doesn't mean you're off course. It means it's time to walk by faith, not by sight. God often goes quiet to grow your trust. He lets you sit in uncertainty so your roots go deeper. He's not punishing you. He's preparing you.

In Exodus, when God led the Israelites out of Egypt, He didn't give them a GPS with turn-by-turn directions. He gave them a cloud by day and fire by night—just enough guidance for the next step.

That's still His style.

Revelation usually comes as daily bread—not a lifetime supply.

So what do you do in the fog?

Keep doing the last thing God told you to do. Go back to the instruction you *did* receive—and keep walking in it. If He hasn't updated the orders, it means they still stand.

Remember what He already said. Go back to your journals. Reread the confirmations. God is not flaky. If He spoke it, He meant it. It's interesting to me how often He extols the power of *remembering* in the scriptures.

Get honest with Him. You don't need to pretend in prayer. Tell Him you're tired. Tell Him you're confused. Tell Him you're still here. That honesty opens the door for deeper intimacy—and often fresh revelation.

Lean on community. God often speaks through people—mentors, friends, leaders, counselors. Don't isolate. Reach out. Someone else may carry the word you need for this season.

God still speaks. The Spirit still whispers. Your mission is still intact—even when you feel off course.

Spiritual Resilience: Living Purpose for the Long Haul

Purpose is not a sprint. It's not a single achievement. It's not a one-season assignment.

Purpose is a lifelong unfolding—a covenant journey you walk with God one faithful step at a time.

And if you're going to live it well, you're going to need resilience. Not just grit. Not just willpower. Spiritual resilience.

Spiritual resilience is the ability to keep showing up in obedience, even when you don't see immediate results. It's trusting the seed is growing, even when the soil looks dead. It's believing that faithfulness matters more than fanfare.

Consider two parents of a teenage son who decided church wasn't for him. Sunday after Sunday, he'd slump on the couch while they got ready. He'd roll his eyes during family prayer. Refuse to read scripture. Shrug off every effort with silence or sarcasm.

Still, they kept inviting. Kept praying. Kept making space for him—not just in their schedule but in their hearts.

For years, it felt like nothing was happening. No breakthrough moment. No prodigal return. Just small gestures of obedience: a seat saved at the table, a quiet text that said "We're here if you want to talk," a light left on late.

And then one night—without warning or fanfare—he came to them. Said he was ready to talk. Ready to try. Not because of one big sermon or some spiritual epiphany, but because, as he put it, "You never gave up on me. Even when I gave up on everything else."

That's spiritual resilience in parenting.

It's not about perfect kids or quick results. It's about faithful presence—the kind that outlasts resistance and makes room for redemption.

This kind of resilience doesn't come from discipline alone. It comes from abiding in Christ.

Abide means to stay, to remain, to dwell.

"I am the vine, ye are the branches . . . without me ye can do nothing" (John 15:5).

Your ability to walk in purpose is directly tied to your intimacy with the Savior. The more rooted you are in Him, the more fruit you'll bear—even in dry seasons. You can't live with clarity or courage if you're cut off from your source. Your calling isn't something you just figure out; it's something you stay connected to through revelation.

So when things get tough—when you feel like your effort isn't making a dent—don't panic. Don't overcorrect. Don't quit.

Just abide.

Go back to Him.

Go back to prayer.

Go back to the Word.

Go back to the last yes.

And trust that heaven is still at work behind the scenes. God doesn't waste obedience. He doesn't forget the offering. He doesn't abandon the ones who step out in faith.

Final Reflection: This Is the Life

You might be tempted to think purpose is something you'll fully step into one day—once the timing is right, once the kids are older, once the money comes through.

But this is it.

Right here. Right now. In this ordinary week with these unfinished tasks and this imperfect faith.

You're not preparing to live your purpose. You're living it right now—in how you show up, how you listen, how you serve, how you stay close to the voice that called you.

We don't just need purpose for the big moments. We need it for the ordinary ones—when no one's clapping, when routines feel stale, when spiritual practices risk becoming just checkboxes. If we forget *why* we're doing what we're doing, we lose more than momentum. We lose meaning. Elder José A. Teixeira spoke directly to this kind of drift, reminding us that purpose—real, spiritual purpose—is sustained by love, not obligation:

> When our lives are filled with purpose and service, we avoid spiritual apathy; on the other hand, when our lives are deprived of divine purpose, meaningful service to others, and sacred opportunities for pondering and reflection, we gradually become suffocated by our own activity and self-interest, risking losing our savor. The antidote to this is to continue to be involved in service—being anxiously engaged in good works and the betterment of ourselves and the society we live in.[42]

When purpose is rooted in love for the Savior, it lasts. It grows. And it transforms even the quietest acts of discipleship into sacred, soul-shaping work.

You don't have to have it all figured out. You just have to stay anchored.

Your Father in Heaven knows exactly what He's doing. And He's not finished with you yet.

7
Designing a Life Around Your Purpose

"The meaning of life is to find your gift. The purpose of life is to give it away." —Pablo Picasso (attributed)[43]

ONCE YOU'VE IDENTIFIED YOUR PURPOSE, THE NEXT BIG STEP IS SIMple to say and hard to do:

Live it.

Not once. Not someday. Every day.

Designing a life around your purpose doesn't mean quitting your job, selling your house, or fleeing to some purpose retreat in the woods (unless you're into that sort of thing). It means building rhythms, routines, and relationships that support the mission God has placed in your heart.

It's about weaving purpose into the ordinary. Your daily actions. Your work. Your family life. Your service. Your schedule.

Because here's the truth: Purpose isn't just something you "find." It's something you live—and that requires intentional design.

A while back, a video popped up on my social media feed that caught my attention. It was this young, energetic pastor with a sweet fauxhawk preaching passionately about one of my favorite scriptures: "For we are his workmanship, created in Christ Jesus unto good works, which God hath before ordained that we should walk in them" (Ephesians 2:10).

He said something to the effect of this: "We don't have to be a superstar, all-star, or MVP, but God has wired you, designed you, and created you with the gifts, and passion, and talents, and abilities for a reason; and maybe your reason isn't to be known, or famous, or to be a Jesus-influencer on Instagram. Maybe the reason He wired you the way you are—with skills in accounting, or woodworking, or landscaping, or clothes-making—is because there is someone in your world who needs to be blessed by what God has put in you."

The video was captioned with these lines: "In other words, saved people serve people. How will you use your God-given gifts and talents to serve others? Where do you think you can start?"

Saved people serve people. I love that.

My friend Kurt Francom said it this way: "God never lives in a smaller story. He literally creates galaxies. And yet, as his children, we can slip into that smaller story from time to time. And when difficulty or trial or affliction hits, if we don't have the bigger purpose, we may stumble."

Looking again at this verse, let's break it down and connect it to the idea of purpose:

"For we are his workmanship"—This phrase reminds us that we are not random creations. We are God's workmanship, meaning that He is the master Creator who has intricately designed us with care and intention. Each of us is uniquely crafted by God, with specific talents, gifts, and potential. Understanding that we are God's workmanship gives us a sense of purpose—we are here for a reason, created by a divine being who knows us personally and has a plan for us.

"Created in Christ Jesus unto good works"—This part of the verse explains *why* we were created—to do good works through Christ. Our purpose isn't just to exist or to focus on ourselves; it's to engage in actions that reflect Christ's example. These "good works" can vary greatly depending on our individual gifts and circumstances, but the key idea is that our lives are meant to be focused outward, serving others, lifting those around us, and contributing to the betterment of the world. Our purpose is aligned with following Christ and becoming instruments in His hands.

"Which God hath before ordained"—This points to the idea that God has a plan for each of us. Even before we were born, God ordained certain works and roles for us to fulfill. This doesn't mean that we are predestined to a rigid path, but rather that God, knowing us perfectly, has laid out opportunities for us to accomplish meaningful things in our lives. Our purpose then is to seek out those divinely ordained opportunities—to follow promptings, make choices in line with God's will, and fulfill the roles He knows we're capable of.

"That we should walk in them"—Finally, this phrase speaks to our responsibility to actively live out our purpose. We aren't just passive participants in life; rather, we are to walk in the good works God has laid before us. To walk in these works means to live with intention, recognizing that our actions, decisions, and relationships are part of our God-given purpose. We are called to walk in alignment with God's plan, constantly seeking to fulfill the unique mission He has for us.

This verse beautifully illustrates that our purpose is rooted in our divine creation. We were made by God, through Christ, with a specific purpose: to do good works that God has prepared for us. Discovering and living our purpose means understanding that we are not random or aimless but that God has shaped us for meaningful roles in His plan. Our purpose is to use the talents and opportunities He has given us to bless others and to align our lives with His will. The call to "walk in them" reminds us that purpose is not just about knowing we were created for a reason but about actively living it out, every day, with faith and trust in God's plan.

So how do you maximize your purpose?

Start where you are. Let me explain.

In the Doctrine and Covenants, God says to be anxiously engaged in a good cause and do many things of our own free will (see Doctrine and Covenants 58:27). What is a good cause? It's your purpose. Find something that brings you purpose and pursue it anxiously.

Many years ago, Yale management professor Amy Wrzesniewski ran an interesting study that highlights the power of purpose.[44] She interviewed hospital custodians to understand what drives job satisfaction, particularly in roles often viewed as undesirable. She found that while some custodians felt unfulfilled, others found meaning and purpose in their work—even though they had the same job, in the same environment, with the same people. The difference was in their personal sense of purpose, which they brought with them to the job.

Some custodians saw their role as simply mopping floors and described their work as monotonous and low-skill. They came in for the paycheck, with little motivation beyond that. Others, however, viewed their work through the lens of their greater purpose. One custodian, for example, saw herself as a "healer," understanding that properly sanitizing hospital rooms was essential to patient safety. She didn't just clean floors—she protected lives. It wasn't the task itself that made the difference; it was her sense of purpose that infused meaning into her job.

These custodians also went beyond their typical job duties in small but meaningful ways, not because it was required but because they felt a deeper responsibility. They found ways to connect with patients, making sure to use cleaning products that wouldn't irritate sensitive individuals, or talking to coma patients to stimulate brain activity. Some even maintained friendships with patients after they left the hospital. These actions were rooted in their purpose to care for others, not because their job demanded it but because they felt it was part of who they were.

The sense of purpose you bring to your work, calling, family, or ministering can transform how you approach it. It's not about finding fulfillment in the work itself but about doing the work as an expression of who you are and what you believe in. While no job, calling, or assignment is perfect, and some challenges are real, having a sense of purpose can help you navigate your responsibilities with greater meaning and motivation.

I would say that there is no job, calling, or assignment that is devoid of purpose. None. But you have to proactively seek to apply your purpose to the work you're doing.

A few years back, I did a podcast on Leading Saints focused on purpose. Afterward, I got an email from a man named Ryan who has since become a close friend. He's a pilot and a bishop in Arizona. He shared about his efforts to mine his past to discover his purpose and told me that growing up, he didn't feel the love he hoped for and needed as a child and youth. He often craved that sense of connection and the feeling of being seen and heard. I asked him how that past informed his decision to be a pilot, and he made an interesting connection.

He said that flying allowed him to show care and compassion to people on his plane and to lift their spirits. He homed in on the statement "I exist to love and lift others." He said that flying allowed him to literally lift others, from one place to another, but also to metaphorically lift others' spirits and to show them kindness as they travel from point A to point B for various purposes—weddings, funerals, vacations, and more.

I asked him how he applies that purpose in his life. He shared that to "love" means to help people feel heard, seen, and cared for, and he uses that purpose to guide his interactions with the youth as a bishop. He shepherds them and helps them identify their talents and God-given gifts. He "lifts" as he meets with people and seeks to elevate their spirits and their vision to a higher plane.

He told me he uses that purpose statement every day in every environment he's in.

See, purpose shifts the way we approach any task. Let's see what this looks like in different spheres of life.

1. Parenting

Without Purpose: A parent might go through the daily motions of getting kids ready for school, making meals, and checking homework in a mechanical way—just crossing off tasks that need to be done. They see it as part of the daily grind.

With Purpose: When a parent understands the deeper purpose of nurturing, teaching, and guiding their children toward growth, these same tasks can become opportunities to bond, to teach life lessons, and to demonstrate love. Preparing a meal is no longer just about food; it's about serving and showing care for the family.

2. Workplace Interaction

Without Purpose: A person may handle an office email or attend meetings with no emotional engagement, just checking off boxes, following protocol, and keeping conversations to a minimum to get back to their "real" tasks.

With Purpose: With purpose, even a simple email becomes a chance to communicate clearly, build relationships, or lift others. The meeting turns into an opportunity to collaborate meaningfully, problem-solve, or improve the environment of the workplace, with a focus on how the interaction can serve others or contribute to a larger mission.

3. Customer Service

Without Purpose: A retail worker could approach every customer interaction as a routine task—scanning items, processing payments, and wishing customers a good day with no genuine care behind it.

With Purpose: When the retail worker understands their purpose as helping to make someone's day better or solving a problem for a customer, their interaction becomes much more personal and thoughtful. A smile, a kind word, or even going the extra mile to help a customer find what they need can transform a job into a meaningful experience.

4. Volunteering

Without Purpose: A volunteer may serve meals at a shelter out of obligation or to get in some service hours, going through the motions and interacting as little as possible.

With Purpose: When they understand that their presence can bring dignity, love, and hope to people in difficult circumstances, they may interact more warmly, ask about people's stories, and engage in meaningful conversation, truly serving with their whole heart.

5. Studying

Without Purpose: A student might study for exams purely out of a sense of obligation, memorizing facts to pass the test and feeling disconnected from the material.

With Purpose: With a sense of purpose, the student could approach studying as a way to gain knowledge that will help them grow, expand their mind, and prepare them to make a meaningful contribution in the world. Each subject becomes part of a larger vision of personal growth and future impact.

6. Cleaning or Maintenance

Without Purpose: A custodian might view their job as simply wiping down surfaces, vacuuming, and throwing away trash—nothing more than manual labor done out of necessity.

With Purpose: With purpose, a custodian might see their work as essential for creating a safe and clean environment, contributing to the well-being of everyone who uses the space. They might take pride in making sure everything is spotless, knowing that their efforts help prevent illness or create a welcoming atmosphere.

7. Teaching

Without Purpose: A teacher might just go through the curriculum, giving lectures, grading papers, and doing what's required to cover the material, feeling detached from their students' experience.

With Purpose: When teaching with purpose, the same teacher might actively engage with their students, understanding that they have the potential to inspire a love of learning, help students see their own potential, and shape their future paths. Every lesson becomes a chance to make a lasting impact on a student's life.

8. Church Service

Without Purpose: A person fulfilling a church calling might attend meetings, plan activities, and carry out responsibilities out of a sense of duty or obligation. They may feel like they're just checking off the boxes, going through the motions without feeling a personal connection.

With Purpose: When the person recognizes the spiritual and eternal purpose behind their calling, the same tasks—teaching a lesson, organizing an event, or ministering to others—become opportunities to strengthen faith, build the kingdom of God, and uplift individuals. Every interaction becomes a way to show love and compassion, and every act of service feels like a meaningful contribution to something much greater. Even small efforts are seen as part of God's work, helping others come unto Christ. As King Benjamin taught, "When ye are in the service of your fellow beings ye are only in the service of your God" (Mosiah 2:17). If you're still unsure of your purpose, start with this: serve. Serve wherever you are, however you can. Because purpose isn't just something you discover—it's something you practice. And it often reveals itself in motion.

In all these examples, purpose turns the task from a "job to be done" into something that holds deeper meaning, influences how we interact with others, and brings a sense of fulfillment. When you recognize the "why" behind your actions, it shifts from being transactional to transformational. And in all activities related to purpose, our ultimate goal is to become like Christ, point others to Him, and feel His love more abundantly. This is the biggest why.

Purpose in the Small Moments

Cole is a great example of the power of spending even one hour exploring your purpose to gain clarity about the future.

When I met Cole at the deli for lunch and asked him how his day was, he exclaimed, "Amazing!" And he actually meant it. He woke up that morning and hit the surf, and the waves were awesome.

Waves? What waves? We live in Houston.

"Yeah, I drove down to Surfside Beach off Galveston and surfed this morning. I love doing that. The cold water, the exercise . . . amazing."

Cole and I got together to figure out his nineteen-year-old life. He wanted to know what he should do for a living. Turns out that the way he spent his morning was pretty instructive.

Cole was an athlete in high school, football and lacrosse primarily, and was on a crash course for engineering—"because I was good in math and science, and from the time I was a kid, everyone around me said I'd be a good engineer."

Then his life changed.

It started when his sister introduced him to rock climbing at a gym. He was instantly hooked and didn't want to do anything else. It was highly technical but low impact, which was important for someone with back pain from lacrosse.

Around the same time, he had a revelation: His self-worth and self-esteem were tied up in external things—relationships, friendships, and what others wanted him to do. In other words, he was making decisions based on extrinsic factors.

He reflected on this, and through a series of failures, books, and mentors, Cole realized that true self-confidence comes from inside, from knowing who you are, giving to others, and showing love.

In quick succession, he went from rock climbing to slacklining to camping and anything else outdoors. He applied and was accepted to a job at a scout ranch in New Mexico, and shortly after, he started teaching classes for kids at a rock-climbing gym, in addition to teaching a "Habits for Life" course to help kids develop the habits that lead to a successful life. "I've always felt connected to the outdoors. That's where I feel most authentic."

He recounted his time in scouting and being in nature. Then I asked him the million-dollar question: "So, if you could do anything for a career, and money wasn't a factor, what would you do?"

"I'm not sure. I wanted to change hearts . . . to build esteem. But I don't know how to do that for a career."

Fair enough. And yet the answer was right there.

It starts with a purpose. In his case, to build others' self-esteem from the inside out.

Now comes the hard part—not getting distracted. See, Cole belongs in a job in the outdoor arena: directing an outdoor adventures office at a college or university, working in the national forest system, leading disabled youth in outdoor learning, coordinating outdoor trips for businesses and other organizations, leading canoeing or white-water rafting trips, and so on.

But somewhere along the line, other tempting career paths will emerge: consulting, law, engineering, or business. These stable, society-approved career paths could easily distract him from his core purpose. But my sense is that Cole will stay true. Really, he was ahead of the game at nineteen years old since he'd taken the time to find this clarity about his career options.

As we grabbed an ice cream cone and wrapped up our conversation, I asked him what he was doing for work right now. He said he just finished up a part-time gig and was in between jobs.

"What were you doing?" I asked.

"Cleaning sailboats on the coast." Learning a new craft. In solitude. Outdoors. Where you can clear your mind. Making things better than they were.

"Of course you were," I said. He was naturally, and even subconsciously, drawn to doing what he loves.

Living with Purpose Is a Daily Practice

You wrote a powerful purpose statement. That's amazing. But now what?

Most people's struggle is not with *believing* in their purpose but with *living it out* in the middle of dishes, deadlines, and discouragement.

This chapter is about taking your purpose off the page and putting it into your actual calendar, your actual habits, your actual life.

It's about the shift from theory to practice.

From "someday" to "right now."

President Dieter F. Uchtdorf once reminded us, "God uses ordinary people to accomplish His extraordinary work."[45] You don't need a perfect résumé or a massive platform to matter. Heaven has a long history of using the unnoticed, the unqualified, and the unnamed. Purpose doesn't start when you get a new title—it starts when you show up with the one you already have.

Purpose in the Mundane

One of the lies we tell ourselves is that purpose has to be big, flashy, and Instagrammable.

But when you approach each day with the mindset that everything you do can contribute to your purpose, the small acts become powerful.

Folding laundry.

Making breakfast.

Responding to emails.

Helping with homework.

Leading a meeting.

Sending an encouraging text.

None of it's glamorous. But all of it can be holy.

Think about how Jesus lived. Sure, there were the headline miracles—feeding five thousand, walking on water, raising the dead. But much of His ministry? Small, simple, daily acts of care.

He sat with individuals. He listened. He blessed. He walked. He wept. He lived His purpose through presence, not performance. If it was good enough for the Savior of the world, it's good enough for you and me.

You don't need a new title or platform to live your purpose. You just need new intention.

Rhythms That Reinforce Your Purpose

Living your purpose isn't about one big moment. It's about micro-decisions repeated over time—rhythms that reinforce what matters most. Author James Clear puts it this way: "Every action you take is a vote for the type of person you wish to become."[46] His research on habit formation shows that consistent, small steps—done daily—shape not just our schedules but our identities. That's exactly how purpose works. You don't become purposeful by writing a mission statement. You become purposeful by aligning your habits with it, one decision at a time.

Everyone's rhythm will look different, but the goal is the same: to create a life where your habits, time, and energy are aligned with your God-given mission.

Here are a few powerful rhythms to consider.

1. *Daily Purpose Check-in*

Start the day connected to your purpose. Before the emails, the carpool line, the meetings—take ten minutes to check in with God and your purpose.

Ask:

- "What does faithfulness look like today?"
- "Who needs me to show up on mission today?"
- "Where do I need to step up or step back?"

Even a short prayer and a review of your purpose statement can reset your whole mindset.

2. *Weekly Purpose Check-In*

Every week, set aside fifteen to thirty minutes to review how you're living your purpose.

Ask:

- Where did I live aligned with my purpose?
- Where did I drift?
- What does next week need from me?

Use this time to journal, pray, repent, celebrate, and plan. Don't wait until burnout hits to reflect. Build this rhythm in now—as an act of stewardship.

3. *Monthly Purpose Reset*

Life shifts fast. Your schedule gets chaotic. Vision drifts. That's normal.

Set a monthly rhythm—maybe the first Sunday of each month—to pause and ask:

- Is my life still supporting my purpose?
- What do I need to let go of?
- What needs to be restored, protected, or pursued?

This is your chance to clean house and realign before small detours become major drift.

Purpose and the Eternal Perspective

Now let's zoom way out.

When you're designing your life, don't just ask, "What's urgent?" Ask, "What will matter in a hundred years?"

You're not just building a calendar. You're building a legacy.

Every sacrifice you make now—the patient parenting, the hard conversations, the quiet faithfulness—it all counts. It all echoes. It all gets recorded in the book of life.

One day, you'll look back and see that the smallest acts made the biggest difference. That the days you felt invisible were building something eternal. That the consistency you offered in obscurity laid a foundation that couldn't be shaken.

For a workshop I teach on "becoming a great developer of people," I start by having participants make a list—in sixty seconds—of as many things as they can that qualify as "short-term sacrifices that yield long-term gains." Things that require some effort now but pay off over time. I'm always impressed by their creativity. I think the record is twenty-five things in sixty seconds, including going to the gym, saving money, getting an education, brushing your teeth, waking up early, parenting, budgeting, and therapy. They also say things like wearing sunscreen, taking the stairs, doing your taxes on time, saying no to dessert, deleting social media apps, putting your laundry away, stretching before a workout, and pretending to like kale (!).

What do they all have in common? It's the stuff that matters most in this life! Education! Family! Healthy teeth and bones! Financial stability! Wellness! These are not necessarily enjoyable and require consistency to work, but they ultimately yield true joy. The same holds true for your purpose. It's often in the simple, daily, and even mundane tasks that we express and align with our purpose.

A purpose-filled life may not always be recognized or rewarded here, but God sees. And heaven never forgets.

Design for the Season You're In

One mistake people make when designing their life around purpose is trying to force a structure that doesn't fit their current season.

A mom with three toddlers at home can't live on the same schedule as a retired missionary couple or a single twenty-something launching a nonprofit.

Purpose is not one-size-fits-all. It's seasonal.

You need to design with grace.

That means asking:

- What does faithfulness look like in *this* season?
- What can I say yes to now without burning out?
- What needs to wait—not forever but for now?

Small. Steady. Sacred.

For example, the mom with three toddlers at home isn't going to have long stretches of quiet time or uninterrupted work hours. Her version of purpose might look like teaching gospel principles during snack time, offering compassion to other exhausted moms, or creating a home where the Spirit can dwell—even if the living room is a mess.

A recently returned missionary might have a wide-open schedule and an eagerness to serve but also a sense of uncertainty about what's next. For them, purpose might mean exploring opportunities aligned with their gifts—volunteering, mentoring youth, or building a skill that will later support their calling.

A full-time caregiver for an aging parent might feel stuck or unseen, but their purpose is alive in those quiet acts of mercy and patience. That sacred stewardship is not a detour—it's discipleship in action.

Your season may shift. Your roles may change. Your capacity may stretch or shrink. But your purpose can live inside all of it—if you give it room to breathe.

Don't Wait for Ideal

You don't need ideal conditions to live intentionally. What you need is a decision. Not a perfect plan. Not a sabbatical or a trust fund or a wide-open calendar. Just a quiet resolve to begin—right where you are, with exactly what you have.

Designing your life around purpose doesn't require a grand unveiling or a dramatic life overhaul. It begins in the ordinary. In fact, the most profound changes often take root in the most unremarkable soil—the morning routine you feel stuck in, the emails you don't want to answer, the meetings that feel repetitive, the home that's more loud than peaceful.

You may be tempted to think you'll start living with purpose once the kids are older. Once the job gets better. Once you're less tired. But the truth is, if you wait for ideal conditions, you'll be waiting your entire life.

You're not waiting on a green light from the universe. You already got the green light from God.

So start where your feet are. Start while it's messy. Start when no one else notices. Start before you feel ready.

Maybe for you, it means building in five minutes of stillness before the house wakes up, not because you're trying to win at morning routines but because you want to reconnect with why any of it matters. Maybe it's choosing to listen more intentionally to your spouse during dinner instead of scrolling in the pause between bites. Maybe it's changing how you approach your work—not by quitting but by infusing your current role with deeper purpose and presence.

Start small. Start scared. Start anyway.

Let your schedule begin to reflect what you truly value. Let your yes mean something. Let your purpose show up not just in the big headline moments but in the *tiny, invisible choices* that make up most of your life.

Final Assignment: Live the Design

You don't need to overhaul your whole life in a weekend. But you do need to own it.

You are not a passive passenger drifting through days. You are a steward of sacred potential. A builder of impact. A cocreator with God in the story He's still writing through you.

And the life you're shaping?

It's not for likes.

It's not for applause.

It's not even for comfort.

It's for eternity.

You're building something that will outlast your job title, your follower count, your net worth, and even your self-doubt. You're building a life of purpose—one aligned, surrendered, faithful day at a time.

Your Assignment

1. **Review your purpose statement.** Revisit what you've written. Read it out loud. Pray over it. Ask God to refine it if needed or reignite it if it's grown stale.
2. **Identify one area of misalignment.** Where in your current rhythm are you out of sync with that purpose? Your work? Your relationships? Your habits? Don't judge it—just name it.
3. **Design one small act of alignment.** What's one intentional step you can take this week to bring your life into closer harmony with your purpose? Think small. Think specific. Think faithful. For example, schedule a thirty-minute block for focused reflection or prayer, reach out to a person you feel nudged to encourage, or say no to something good so you can say yes to something aligned. Begin reshaping how you show up in a routine task—doing it with purpose rather than autopilot.
4. **Commit to rhythm, not perfection.** You're not trying to live every hour on mission. You're building a rhythm—a sustainable pattern of intentionality that fits your season and strengthens your spirit.
5. **Write a three- to four-sentence "Purpose Manifesto."** Declare what you're building and why. Write it somewhere visible—on your mirror, your phone, or your desk—as a daily reminder of who you are and what you're called to do.

Don't wait for perfect timing or guaranteed success. Start building. Start aligning. Start living your purpose.

8
When the Dream Doesn't Match the Data: Trusting Purpose Through Disappointment

"Disappointment is a kind of bankruptcy—the bankruptcy of a soul that expends too much in hope and expectation." —Eric Hoffer[47]

YOU FINALLY GOT CLARITY ON YOUR PURPOSE.

You prayed. You journaled. You wrote the statement. You felt the fire.

You stepped forward in faith—maybe you started the thing, applied for the position, opened your mouth, sent the pitch, created the space.

You were expecting fruit. Momentum. Confirmation.

Instead?

Crickets. Or worse—resistance, rejection, failure, silence.

And that sinking feeling started creeping in: Did I miss it?

Because here's what no one tells you in the social media highlight reels and spiritual TED Talks:

There will be moments when the *dream* doesn't match the *data*.

Moments when your purpose feels more like a punchline than a promise.

Moments when you want to scream, "God, where are You?"

This chapter is for those moments.

The Gap Between Calling and Results

Let's name the pain.

You felt called to lead—but the people didn't follow.

You felt called to create—but no one bought the thing.

You felt called to teach—but the room was empty.

You felt called to start the program—but it tanked.

You felt called to share your story—but all you got was silence.

That gap between what you *thought* would happen and what *actually* happened? That's the ache of disappointment. It's the part we skip over too often in church talks and podcasts. But it's part of every real calling.

Every. Single. One.

Moses. Joseph. Esther. Alma. Abinadi. Mary. Peter. Paul. Nephi. Jesus.

All of them experienced that gap.

They were called—and then misunderstood. Rejected. Mocked. Blocked. Abandoned.

The dream was real. But the data didn't match up—at least not right away.

If you're in that space, you're in good company.

The Wait Is Not a Waste

Let's talk about Sarah.

She felt called to help women heal from trauma. She knew it. Felt it in her bones. Wrote it in her journal. Got confirmation after confirmation.

So she launched a website. Wrote a blog. Created resources. Shared her heart.

And almost nothing happened.

No signups. No applause. No wave of changed lives.

What did come was discouragement, financial pressure, impostor syndrome, and a whole lot of second-guessing.

"I thought I heard God," she told me. "Now I just feel embarrassed."

But here's what I told her—and what I'll tell you too: Your obedience is not a failure just because the results don't match your timeline.

Sarah thought she was planting a ministry. But really? She was being planted.

In that season of disappointment, her roots grew deeper. She found her real voice—not the one shaped by fear of failure but by faithfulness.

When she relaunched a year later, the soil was ready. And this time, it bore fruit.

But even if it hadn't, the first step still mattered. Because in God's economy, obedience is success.

Faithfulness ≠ Fast

This is where we have to get real about what purpose looks like.

Faithfulness isn't fast. It's not flashy. It doesn't always trend. It's usually quiet, gritty, unglamorous, and slow.

If you've ever felt like you weren't the smartest person in the room, or like someone else was more naturally gifted, here's some liberating news: Talent isn't the most reliable predictor of success. Not in school. Not in sports. Not in purpose.

Angela Duckworth, a psychologist and former middle school math teacher, spent years trying to figure out what separated high achievers from everyone else. It wasn't IQ. It wasn't social intelligence. And it wasn't access to money or resources.

It was grit.

Duckworth defines grit as "passion and perseverance for long-term goals." In her bestselling book *Grit: The Power of Passion and Perseverance*, she explains that the people who achieve the most—in everything from West Point training to national spelling bees to entrepreneurial ventures—aren't always the most talented. They're the ones who *keep showing up*. Who get knocked down and still keep going. Who remain stubbornly loyal to a calling even when it's not producing immediate results.

That sounds a lot like the kind of spiritual resilience required to walk in purpose.

Grit doesn't mean never struggling. It doesn't mean never doubting or never failing. It means you don't give the struggle the final word. It means you stay in the game when it's boring, when it's costly, when you've seen zero fruit and all the doors seem closed. Duckworth puts it this way: "Enthusiasm is common. Endurance is rare."

And while her research wasn't spiritually framed, it echoes a deeply spiritual principle: Faithfulness over time is what matters most to God. In the parable of the talents, the Master doesn't praise the servant for *how much* he produced—He praises him for being faithful. Jesus doesn't ask for perfect performance. He asks for perseverance.

What's powerful about Duckworth's work is that she found that grit can be developed. It's not a fixed trait. People become gritty when they commit to something they deeply care about and when they give themselves permission to fail without quitting. Purpose actually fuels grit—because when you know *why* you're doing something, it's easier to endure the *how*.

This is good news for anyone who feels disqualified by their limitations. Grit doesn't care how gifted you are. It cares how committed you are.

So the next time you feel discouraged because your purpose feels heavy or hard or slow, remember this: Grit is your superpower. And it's one that heaven honors. Staying power beats spotlight every time.

Keep showing up. Keep believing. Keep pressing forward when it would be easier to retreat.

God doesn't need you to be flawless.

He just needs you to stay in it.

Ask Noah. He built a boat with no water in sight.

Ask Nephi. He built a ship without knowing where it was going.

Ask Alma. He preached to people who stoned him and ran him out of town.

Ask Joseph Smith. He restored the gospel and spent most of his adult life in courtrooms, jail cells, and hiding.

What did they have in common?

They kept showing up. They trusted the One who called them—even when the evidence didn't add up. And eventually, the fruit came. But not before the faith.

Walking Through Disappointment With God

If you're in that place right now—when the fruit isn't visible, the doors aren't opening, and your soul feels bruised—don't fake your way through it.

God doesn't need your performance. He wants your presence. So get real with Him. Tell Him what hurts. Tell Him what doesn't make sense. Tell Him what you hoped for and what you're still holding on to by a thread. Scripture is full of this kind of raw prayer. David. Jeremiah. Job. Even Jesus in Gethsemane.

This isn't a lack of faith.

This *is* faith—trusting God with your full truth.

And in that place, something holy happens.

The disappointment doesn't magically vanish, but it gets held by a God who knows how to sit with sorrow and by a Savior who didn't just bleed for your sin but also for your *disillusionment.*

Your unmet expectations are not too heavy for Him.

What to Do When You're Stuck

If you've ever tried to live your purpose and then hit a wall, you're not broken—you're in good company. Every major figure in scripture, every leader you respect, every faithful servant of God has spent time in the in-between. That foggy middle ground between calling and clarity. Between the dream and the data. It's that moment when you've stepped out in faith, done the thing, obeyed the prompting—and all you hear is silence.

Moses had a clear mission—to lead Israel out of Egypt. But then he hit the wilderness, wandering for forty years, surrounded by whining, doubt, and dust. Joseph had a vision—his brothers would bow to him—but spent years in prison with no evidence that God was still writing the story. Even John the Baptist, the very voice crying in the wilderness to prepare the way for the Messiah, ended up sitting in a jail cell asking, "Art thou he that should come, or do we look for another?" (Matthew 11:3).

Getting stuck doesn't mean you got it wrong. It often means God is doing something deeper than you expected. If you find yourself in that space—the uncomfortable waiting room between obedience and outcome—here are four things that can help you stay grounded.

1. Go Back to Your Last Clear Yes

When we feel disoriented, our instinct is often to scramble for new instructions. We beg God for a fresh word. A new confirmation. A breakthrough. And sometimes He gives it. But more often, what we need isn't something new—it's a return to what we already know.

What was the last thing God clearly told you to do? Go back to that. Revisit the moment He confirmed your direction, your purpose, your identity. That clarity didn't expire just because things got hard. God is not flippant with His voice. He doesn't change His mind just because you're in a holding pattern. If He hasn't spoken something new, it's usually because the last thing still stands.

One of the enemy's oldest tricks is to sow doubt in the middle of delay. "Did God really say . . . ?" That's what he whispered to Eve. And it's still the line he uses on us when time stretches out longer than we hoped. When you're unsure what to do next, don't chase the next shiny thing. Just keep doing the last thing with faithfulness.

2. Reframe the Purpose of the Delay

We tend to see delays as divine silence or punishment—like maybe we didn't pray hard enough, believe big enough, or perform well enough. But more often than not, the delay is part of the design.

Sometimes the pause is there to protect you. Sometimes it's to prepare you. Sometimes it's both. God sees the full picture, and He knows what your purpose will require down the road—strength, resilience, humility, relational maturity—and He'll use the waiting to build it into you.

When David was anointed king, he didn't march to the throne the next morning. He went back to tending sheep. Then came Goliath. Then came Saul's jealousy. Then came years of running, hiding, fighting. It took more than a decade for the promise to turn into a position. But during that delay, God was forming the kind of man who could carry the crown without losing his soul.

So instead of asking, "Why am I stuck?" ask, "What is this delay developing in me?" That one shift can turn a frustrating detour into sacred preparation.

3. Steward What's in Front of You

When purpose feels stalled, we tend to look ahead, scanning the horizon for something big to fix it. But more often than not, God's next step for you is already right in front of you—in the ordinary, the overlooked, the small thing that doesn't look impressive but matters deeply.

I've coached plenty of people who said, "I'm ready for the big thing—the platform, the influence, the calling," while simultaneously ignoring the people and priorities God had already placed in their lap.

Jesus taught us not to despise small beginnings. In fact, the kingdom of heaven often *starts* small—a mustard seed, a few loaves and fish, a widow's mite. If you're faithful in little, you'll be trusted with much (see Luke 16:10). That's not just a principle—it's a pattern.

Ask yourself: Who needs my presence right now? What small task needs my excellence? What habit needs consistency? What prayer needs persistence? You don't need a stage to steward what God's given you. You just need a willing heart and a little attention to the moment you're in.

4. Keep Showing Up

When you're in the gap, showing up feels pointless. The work feels invisible. The prayers feel unanswered. The habits feel unrewarded. But I promise you—they are not wasted.

Every act of obedience is forming something in you. Your consistency is building spiritual muscle. Your character is being tested and refined. Your faith is being strengthened in ways you won't fully understand until you look back.

God is not looking for flashy. He's looking for faithful. The Lord gave a promise in Doctrine and Covenants 64:33: "Be not weary in well-doing, for ye are laying the foundation of a great work. And out of small things proceedeth that which is great." Faithfulness in the unseen places—in the hard, slow, unglamorous moments—is never wasted. You're building something bigger than you can currently see. The prophet Jeremiah preached for forty years with very little visible success. Noah built a boat for a flood no one believed in. Ruth stayed with Naomi without knowing Boaz was around the corner. Showing up, day after day, when no one else sees it—that's where legacy is born.

You may not see fruit yet. But your roots are growing deeper. And what's being developed underground will sustain you when the season of visible fruit comes.

Final Reflection: Your Purpose Is Not a Performance

There's a trap we rarely see coming. It's subtle, even noble-sounding. But it steals joy, breeds anxiety, and eventually hollows out your purpose until it feels like an exhausting performance instead of a sacred calling.

It's the belief that your purpose is measured by applause.

You start with the right motives. You want to make a difference. You want to be obedient. You want to follow God's will. But somewhere along the way, your focus drifts. You start paying attention to metrics—to how many people notice, how much traction you're getting, how fast the fruit shows up.

And when the applause doesn't come, or when the results don't match the effort, you begin to question the whole thing. "If this were really my purpose, wouldn't it be working by now? Wouldn't people be responding? Wouldn't it feel more successful?"

It's a slow erosion of the soul—and it's built on a lie.

Your purpose was never about applause. It was about alignment.

God didn't call you to perform. He called you to follow.

God doesn't grade your purpose like an Instagram algorithm. He's not watching your analytics. He's watching your obedience.

Fruitfulness is often out of your control. But faithfulness? That's yours to give.

The dream God gave you is still alive—even if the data isn't lining up just yet. Your obedience still matters—even when you can't see the outcome. Your calling is still real—even when you're walking through a season that feels more like dying than being born.

So take a deep breath. Lift your head. You're not behind. You're not broken. You're not disqualified. You're simply walking through the quiet, holy middle where God does His best work.

And He's not finished.

Not with your story. Not with your impact. Not with the purpose He placed inside you.

So keep walking.

One step. One "yes." One act of faith at a time.

God's not done.

And neither are you.

9

Multiplying Purpose: Creating Ripple Effects That Last

"What we do now echoes in eternity." —Marcus Aurelius[48]

The real power of purpose isn't found in what you build but in what outlives you.

When I began my study of purpose, I immediately leapt to God's purpose, which is often quoted. I cited it at the beginning of this book, and it's one of maybe three scriptures most Church members know by heart (aside from 1 Nephi 3:7 and "my father dwelt in a tent"): "For behold, this is my work and my glory—to bring to pass the immortality and eternal life of man" (Moses 1:39). God's purpose is clear. He wants to make us immortal and bring us all home to become like Him. What a powerful statement! What a legacy. God wants what we all want for our children—for them to become like God and have everything He has promised.

In 2015, Elder D. Todd Christofferson offered this summary of the Lord's purpose:

> It is important to recognize that God's ultimate purpose is our progress. His desire is that we continue "from grace to grace, until [we receive] a fulness" of all He can give. That requires more than simply being nice or feeling spiritual. It requires faith in Jesus Christ, repentance, baptism of water and of the Spirit, and enduring in faith to the end. One cannot fully achieve this in isolation, so a major reason the Lord has a church is to create a community of Saints that will sustain one another in the "strait and narrow path which leads to eternal life."[49]

God's purpose merits a book of its own, but for now it's sufficient to understand that He has a clear purpose—our progress.

We also have a clear purpose, and one that will outlive us.

It's easy to get fixated on the front-end of purpose—discovering it, defining it, starting to live it. But the long game? That's about multiplication. It's about what happens when your faithfulness outlasts your presence. When the choices you make today echo into eternity—and into lives you may never meet.

Legacy is not some abstract concept for wealthy families and historical figures. Legacy is purpose that ripples. It's your impact, passed on. Multiplied. Carried forward.

And here's the truth: Everyone leaves a legacy. The question is whether it's intentional.

You don't have to be famous to leave a legacy. You just have to be faithful. You already are, in fact. Whether you realize it or not, you're planting seeds every single day. In your family. Your church. Your neighborhood. Your team. Even your social media feed.

The way you respond to disappointment. The way you show up when no one thanks you. The way you raise your kids. The way you speak about other people. It all forms the ripple.

A life of purpose, well-lived, becomes contagious. It catches fire in others. That's exactly what legacy is. It's purpose catching fire—not because you shouted louder but because you burned longer.

Purpose Multiplies Through People, Not Just Platforms

One of the biggest lies of our culture is that impact comes from visibility. That if you're not reaching thousands, you're not really making a difference. That if your name isn't on a podcast or a building, you're doing something wrong. I've certainly felt this self-imposed pressure in the process of building my business. I've wondered if I should go all in on social media, produce a podcast, and blast my name out there to increase my impact. I've wondered if I should become an influencer, producing daily content and becoming a go-to guru. Alas, I continue to feel that the greatest impact I'll ever have will be one-on-one, a conversation at a time.

Some of the most world-changing ripples start with one conversation. One act of courage. One moment of obedience. When you live your purpose faithfully—even quietly—it multiplies through people.

Think about it. Jesus poured the majority of His time into twelve people. And one of those guys completely bailed on Him. But the rest? They carried the message. They carried the mission, and they multiplied it. And now, that message positively impacts approximately 2.3 billion Christians worldwide, representing about 29 percent of the global population. I can imagine that the influencers of His day may have wondered why the Savior wasn't more public, more focused on building His brand or broadcasting His message. It seems that the Savior's approach was more individual—true conversion—and that the ripple effect of one life changed was enough. Imagine the impact of a converted person in all directions—on their ancestry, their family, and their future posterity. The worth of a soul is truly great in the sight of God! (See Doctrine and Covenants 18:10.)

You don't need a bigger audience. You need deeper presence.

Look at your life right now: Who are the people God has already placed around you? Who's watching you, learning from you, being shaped by how you live, how you love, and how you lead?

Your kids.

Your coworkers.

Your Sunday School class.

Your best friend who's hanging on by a thread.

Your younger sibling who watches everything you do.

The teenager in your ward who thinks no one sees him.

The coworker who laughs at your faith but keeps asking you questions.

The neighbor who says she doesn't believe in God but always opens the door when you bring banana bread.

They are your platform.

Don't wait for a bigger one. You don't multiply purpose by going viral. You multiply it by going deep—with the people right in front of you.

Legacy Starts at Home

One of the greatest ripple effects of purpose is what it creates in your family—and not just through some formal devotional or perfectly-scripted family night. Often, it's through quiet modeling. The way you carry yourself. The way you repent. The way you talk about God when the bills are tight and your prayers aren't answered yet. In fact, as I meet with and minister to youth in my calling, I often find that the moments that lead to their conversion are the consistent, even unimpressive, habits that form their family's foundation. They choose to serve a mission because their parent talked about their mission often, or they decide to go to the temple because their parent frequently attended.

I'm inspired by a woman I know who has attended the temple with her kids to do temple baptisms every Friday for at least the past four years. Her children are home-schooled and have some flexibility in their schedule, and she felt that the greatest contribution she could make to their lives each week was to ensure they were in the house of the Lord serving their ancestors. They began attending when I was serving as an ordinance worker in the baptistry, and we built a friendship. I've since watched the group expand from just her children to other youth in the ward and stake. Now, each Friday at 10 a.m., you can expect to see a group of anywhere between ten and twenty-five youth and their parents show up at the Houston temple to do baptisms for their ancestors, and the results have been amazing. Her oldest son is currently serving a mission, while her other kids are also "all in" with the gospel. They are truly converted, and they shine!

This is the power of purpose and legacy. A purpose-filled life teaches your children more than a thousand lectures ever could.

I've worked with so many parents who feel like they've "lost the plot"—like they aren't doing enough for the kingdom because they're knee-deep in carpools, laundry, and Band-Aids. But purpose isn't paused just because your kids need snacks or the house is loud. In fact, that's often where it's most powerfully lived.

Because when your children see you choosing integrity when no one's watching . . .

When they watch you walk through hard seasons without letting bitterness win . . .

When they see you serve someone who can't give anything back . . .

When they watch you worship through your own disappointment . . .

That becomes part of their inheritance.

You don't just leave behind financial assets. You leave behind a spiritual example.

That's legacy.

What you model is what they'll remember. What you practice is what they'll repeat. What you value is what they'll carry forward—long after you're gone.

A Ripple You'll Never Fully See

The beauty and heartbreak of purpose is that much of your impact will unfold after you're gone—or outside your view. Someone you helped will help someone else. A word you spoke will come back to someone at the exact moment they needed it. A small act of obedience will open a door that leads to someone else's miracle.

You may never get to see the full ripple. But you don't need to. Your job isn't to measure impact. It's to multiply faithfulness.

Keep the Fire Burning

You're not here just to live with purpose.

You're here to multiply it.

To hand it off.

To light the next torch.

To become the kind of person who makes other people more alive.

In a world constantly tempting us to self-focus and overcommit, Brother Randall L. Ridd offers this powerful reminder:

> If we are focused on the things of the world, we can miss a whole spiritual world that is all around us. We may not be able to recognize the spiritual promptings that the Holy Ghost is anxious to give us to direct our lives and to bless others. Conversely, if we focus on the things of the Spirit and that which is "virtuous, lovely, or of good report or praiseworthy" (Articles of Faith 1:13), then we're less likely to be sidetracked by the temptations and distractions of the world. The best way to avoid distractions is to have our focus firmly set on our purpose and be anxiously engaged in a good cause. Be careful of your focus—don't spend time focused on climbing a mountain only to discover you have climbed the wrong one.[50]

So keep going. Keep pouring. Keep showing up.
Let your purpose become someone else's permission.
Because that ripple?
It's already moving.

10

Leading with Purpose: Turning Calling into Influence

"The successes in life of those we assist, sponsor, mentor, and lift as they pursue their own talents can bring us great joy and satisfaction." —*Elder Ronald A. Rasband*[51]

Some people believe that purpose is only personal—something you carry within you like a quiet fire, a private conviction. And while that's true to an extent, it's not the full story. Because when your purpose is rooted in something higher than your own ambition—when it's grounded in divine calling—it will not remain private for long. It will ripple outward. It will start shaping your relationships, your decisions, and especially how you lead. True purpose inevitably scales beyond the individual. It becomes influence.

Purpose doesn't just call us forward; it calls others forward too. When you embrace your purpose, even in small and seemingly mundane ways, you become a leader—whether you asked for it or not. And that's the beauty of it. Leadership isn't limited to those with formal titles or corporate authority. It can be found in the actions of a parent raising a child, a Relief Society teacher planning a lesson, a high school student mentoring a peer, or a volunteer coordinating a community project. Leadership, at its root, is influence. And when your influence is shaped by divine purpose, your leadership becomes transformational.

In fact, I've found that some of the most meaningful leadership roles aren't ones we chase—they're the ones that chase us. In my own life, I never set out to be a stake president or start a leadership business. In a recent conversation, I reflected that many leadership opportunities in my life felt accidental on the surface—but unmistakably divine in retrospect. That's how calling often works. It doesn't shout. It whispers through doors quietly opened.

Shortly after being sustained as stake president, I felt strongly impressed that our stake needed a shared sense of mission—something that would help guide every calling, every meeting, and every heart. As I pondered, a phrase kept coming to mind: "The most welcoming and friendly stake in Zion." That became our purpose statement. We would become a place where anyone could show up and feel like they belonged. A place where love wasn't conditional on background, worthiness, or appearance. A place that reflected the radical inclusivity of the Savior Himself.

When I shared that purpose with our members, the results were immediate and powerful. People caught the vision. One sister described how her entire class dynamic shifted as girls began connecting more deeply. Others noted how they came early to church—not just to sit but to greet and welcome. Ministering increased. Ward councils got more intentional. And we started hearing stories—powerful stories—about individuals who had been inactive for years feeling prompted to return, and when they did, they were embraced. Not judged. Not scrutinized. Just welcomed. Just loved. That's the power of purpose in leadership. It multiplies.

The difference between positional power and purpose-driven leadership is profound. Positional leaders rely on their role, their authority, and the systems that give them influence. They often lead from above—managing, instructing, controlling. Purpose-driven leaders, on the other hand, lead from within. They don't need the spotlight.

Their authority comes from clarity—clarity about who they are, what they stand for, and why they're leading in the first place. This is the kind of leadership that produces not just compliance but commitment. Not just performance but transformation.

Purpose-driven leaders also let go of the need to meet everyone else's expectations. It's liberating to realize that God isn't asking us to perform in our callings—He is asking us to obey. When your leadership is shaped by what God is asking of you, rather than what others expect from you, you start leading with authenticity instead of anxiety.

One of the most powerful examples of purpose-driven leadership comes from the life of Jesus Christ. In John 13, we find Him at the Last Supper, fully aware that His hour had come. The text tells us, "Jesus knowing that the Father had given all things into his hands . . . riseth from supper, and laid aside his garments; and took a towel, and girded himself" (John 13:3–4). What follows is perhaps one of the most humble and striking moments in all of scripture: The Savior of the world kneels to wash the feet of His disciples. He knew His mission. He knew His divine identity. And from that place of clarity and security, He served. That's what real leadership looks like—not self-promotion but self-emptying. Not dominance but devotion.

President Howard W. Hunter once said, "The world in which we live would benefit greatly if men and women everywhere would exercise the pure love of Christ, which is kind, meek, and lowly."[52] That kind of love-infused leadership—the kind that elevates and empowers rather than controls—is what the Savior modeled. It's also what He invites us to emulate.

When we lead from purpose, we lead from identity. We don't need constant validation because we already have confirmation. And that kind of leadership is deeply resilient. It doesn't depend on circumstances going well or people applauding. It anchors itself in obedience, not outcomes. So when the ward gets split, or your project fails, or no one shows up to the event you planned with your whole heart, you don't quit. You don't spiral. You remember your why. You remember your calling. You remember who sent you.

Purpose in leadership is also about vision—helping others see what they can become and where they're headed. It means you aren't just managing behaviors or metrics. You're nurturing growth. You're seeing people as God sees them: as eternal beings with divine potential. You aren't merely coordinating tasks. You're cultivating purpose in others. This doesn't always look dramatic. Sometimes it's as simple as well-timed encouragement or a quiet act of faithfulness. But it adds up. It changes lives.

This kind of leadership—rooted in divine purpose—requires patience. It takes faith to lead when you don't see immediate results. But spiritual resilience is forged in those moments. Doctrine and Covenants 81:5 gives us a sacred blueprint: "Wherefore, be faithful; stand in the office which I have appointed unto you; succor the weak, lift up the hands which hang down, and strengthen the feeble knees." That's what leadership rooted in purpose looks like. It is faithful. It is steady. It is others-focused.

I often use the image of a full cup with just one more drop. When you're living a life full of good things but not anchored in purpose, that one more responsibility can feel like the thing that breaks you. But when you're living from overflow—when your cup is overflowing with clarity and connection to God—that same drop doesn't feel like a burden. It becomes part of your offering.

In my coaching work with leaders—across businesses, schools, churches, and nonprofits—I've seen the difference purpose makes. Leaders who operate from a deep sense of calling navigate challenges with greater clarity and peace. They inspire trust because people sense their authenticity. They're not leading for personal gain. They're leading because they believe in something bigger than themselves. That kind of leadership is magnetic. It draws others in. It invites them to consider their own purpose, to reflect on their own calling.

Jesus reminded His disciples, "He that is greatest among you, let him be as the younger; and he that is chief, as he that doth serve" (Luke 22:26). Leadership in the kingdom of God is never about climbing over others. It's about stooping to lift. It's about using influence not to elevate yourself but to elevate others.

This is especially true in Church settings. In an interview for the Leading Saints podcast, I mentioned how one of the most powerful tools a Primary president or ward council can use is purpose. When a leader helps their team clarify why they exist—what their shared divine assignment is—they begin to function less like a group of volunteers and more like a body of believers. When a branch presidency leads from purpose, they stop simply planning activities and start guiding transformation. The shift is subtle, but the results are significant.

But what happens when a purpose-driven leader struggles? What happens when the vision grows dim or the influence feels small? These are real questions. And the answer isn't to perform more or shout louder. The answer is to return to the source. Purpose-driven leaders regularly reconnect with their spiritual roots. They pray. They study. They remember the promises made in quiet moments of revelation. They lead from overflow, not depletion. They understand that leadership is not just a job; it's a sacred stewardship.

We need more leaders like that—especially now. Leaders who serve without striving. Who speak with conviction, not condemnation. Who can hold space for both grace and accountability. And who are more concerned with being faithful than being famous. These are the leaders who will shape the future of the Church, the workplace, and the world.

So how do we become these kinds of leaders? We start by identifying how our personal purpose intersects with the needs of others. We ask questions like "Where has God placed me? Who has He called me to serve? What strengths do I have that can bless others?" These questions lead us not to selfish ambition but to sacred responsibility.

Every one of us has a mission here on earth, and every calling we receive is a part of it, no matter how seemingly big or small. When we begin to shift our approach to a calling from something we "do" to who we are *becoming* through serving, our service is amplified and lives are touched.

Lately in our stake, I've felt inspired to reinforce a teaching from Elder Steven Shumway from the 2025 general conference. He said the following:

> We may be more concerned with a culture of performance than with the doctrine of progression, neglecting to see how the Savior increases capacity in the unlikely and the unproven by giving them opportunities to serve.

> If Christ were physically here, He would visit the sick, teach the Sunday School class, sit with the heartbroken young woman, and bless the children. He can do His own work. But He lives this principle of letting us act and learn, so He sends us in His place.[53]

Each calling is an opportunity to become more like Him. These responsibilities are less about our performance (we're not chasing results) and more about our growth. I've had to let go of my tendency as a professional organizational consultant to want to improve the efficiency of the stake as if it were an organization to be improved. Instead, knowing that the Lord can do His own work (see 2 Nephi 27:20), I now view the role of the wards and stake as providing opportunities for members to serve one another, develop Christlike attributes, and become more like the Savior, regardless of outcomes or results.

Leading with purpose means keeping in mind this greater vision.

We also lead with intentional habits. We build rhythms of reflection, service, and connection into our daily lives. We don't wait for big moments. We lead with consistency in small ones. We hold ourselves accountable—not to perfection but to presence. We show up. We listen. We encourage. We lead.

Leadership is not about becoming the Savior. It's about pointing people to Him. It's about becoming so anchored in our own purpose that others feel safe enough to pursue theirs. It's about multiplying faith. Igniting hope. Embodying love. That's what legacy looks like. And it begins with purpose.

I remember serving as a branch president several years ago and learning this important lesson. I was doing my best to counsel members through very challenging situations and felt totally inadequate doing so. I was getting worn down and discouraged. I visited with our stake president at the time and shared my weakness. He challenged me with an interesting thought: "Perhaps you are getting discouraged because these members' problems aren't yours to solve, but you're trying to solve them."

Wait, if they're not mine to solve as the *branch president,* whose are they to solve?

"They're the Lord's to solve," he said. "He knows them better than anyone and knows exactly how to help them move forward. Just point them to the Savior and let Him do His work."

Point them to Him. He will help them fulfill their purpose.

In the end, purpose in leadership is not about how many people follow you. It's about how faithfully you follow the One who called you. That's the kind of leadership that matters. That's the kind that lasts.

And that's the kind the world is waiting for.

11

Commissioned: Being Sent on Purpose, with Purpose

"You are a son or daughter of God with unlimited, divine potential. . . . Your task is to let your true identity as a child of God shape the decisions you make now and for eternity." —President Russell M. Nelson[54]

This book was never meant to be a pep talk. It wasn't designed to give you a quick hit of inspiration only to have you fall back into routine. It was meant to prepare you for movement. If you're holding these pages, it's likely because something in your spirit whispered that there was more. You felt the tug—the sense that life, as it stands, is not all there is. And you wanted to name that. So you did.

You've traveled a journey—sometimes inward, sometimes upward. You've remembered your divine identity. You've examined your story and seen the fingerprints of God in places both joyful and jagged. You've faced your fears, written your purpose statement, and begun to glimpse what a life of intention might look like. But all of that was preparation. Now the call shifts. This is the part where you begin to move.

It's a shift from preparation to commission. From pondering to stepping. From receiving to responding. Because God never reveals purpose for entertainment. He reveals it for assignment. This is how He has always worked. Throughout scripture and across the sacred arc of your own life, God first speaks—then sends.

Moses had the burning bush. Then came Pharaoh.

Esther received insight. Then came the fast.

Nephi heard the Spirit. Then began the journey.

Joseph Smith saw the vision. Then came years of hardship.

Even the Savior—after His baptism came the wilderness, and after the wilderness came the ministry.

Revelation is never the end. It's the catalyst. It awakens something inside that demands movement. Clarity leads to calling. Identity births obedience. The same is true for you.

This is not a time to stay idle or wait for permission. This is your sending. Being sent doesn't mean you're flawless or ready by the world's standards. It means that God trusts you with something holy. You may still feel like you're fumbling, uncertain, or underqualified—but you carry within you a message, a mission, a light. And that light is not yours to hoard.

Jesus didn't wait to send His disciples until they were polished. He sent them while they were still raw—still full of questions and insecurities. Because the power was never in their credentials; it was in the message they carried. The same is true of you. God has placed you where you are—in your home, your city, your calling, your relationships—because your presence matters. Your impact matters. Your obedience, offered even imperfectly, will ripple in ways you may never see.

Don't wait to feel fearless. Don't wait for perfect clarity. Start where you are. This isn't about doing everything at once. It's about stepping into the next right thing—the thing you already feel prompted to begin. It could be mentoring a teenager, initiating a conversation, stepping up in your calling, starting that creative project, or showing up in your home with renewed love and focus.

Every movement matters. Every act of obedience contributes to the mission. Purpose is never fulfilled in theory. It's lived in motion.

But let's not pretend this is easy. Being sent comes with a cost. It will ask something of you—your comfort, your control, maybe even your reputation. You will face resistance. People may misunderstand. You might have to say no to things that used to define you or yes to things that scare you. And you'll wonder, at times, whether it's worth it.

But here's the truth I've learned in my own life—and seen echoed in the lives of the thousands I've coached and walked with:

Obedience costs something. But disobedience always costs more.

There is a unique ache that comes from resisting your purpose. It's the weight of knowing you were made for more but staying stuck in fear. It's the dull pain of playing small when something inside you longs to rise. And once you've glimpsed what God is inviting you into, that ache won't let you go. It's mercy, really—a holy discomfort designed to push you forward.

You weren't created for ease. You were created for glory. Not the kind of glory the world hands out, but the kind that comes from walking in the fullness of your design. The kind that shines through quiet obedience, costly love, and faith that keeps showing up.

Glory isn't found in applause. It's found in surrender.

You've walked this journey of purpose. You've asked the hard questions. You've named your fears and faced down your villains. You've begun designing a life that reflects your mission. And now? Now you step into your commission.

This isn't about becoming someone new. It's about walking in the truth of who you've always been—a child of God, fully equipped, wholly loved, and strategically placed.

You are sent.

To speak with courage.

To serve with humility.

To lead with conviction.

To love without limits.

To live on purpose—in every role, every space, every season.

You don't go alone. The same Spirit that called you will go with you. You don't go unequipped. Grace will meet you with every step.

You don't go unseen. Heaven is watching and cheering and backing every move.

President Ezra Taft Benson put it best when he said, "Men and women who turn their lives over to God will discover that He can make a lot more out of their lives than they can. He will deepen their joys, expand their vision, quicken their minds, strengthen their muscles, lift their spirits, multiply their blessings, increase their opportunities, comfort their souls, raise up friends, and pour out peace. Whoever will lose his life in the service of God will find eternal life."[55]

Likewise, President Russell M. Nelson testified, "You can help shape the destiny of the entire human family! You and your fellow Saints will be scattered like seeds in the wind to build up the Church in all parts of the world. As you know and apply the teachings of the Lord in your life and in your work, you can change the world. You will become a precious part of His perennial pattern: the Lord uses the unlikely to accomplish the impossible!"[56]

This is your threshold moment. The fire is in you now. You've been awakened for impact. The world is waiting for your story—lived fully, offered freely, and surrendered completely.

So go.

And don't look back.

Notes

1. "The State of the Church 2018," Barna, Apr. 17, 2018, https://www.barna.com/research/state-church-2018/.
2. Alan T. Phillips, "God Knows and Loves You," *Liahona*, Nov. 2023, 49.
3. "He Who Has a Why," Goodreads, accessed Aug. 1, 2025, https://www.goodreads.com/quotes/137-he-who-has-a-why-to-live-for-can-bear.
4. Bruce R. McConkie, *The Mortal Messiah: From Bethlehem to Calvary* (Deseret Book, 1979), 1:23, 25.
5. William Damon, *The Path to Purpose: Helping Our Children Find Their Calling in Life* (Free Press, 2008), 33.
6. Angela Duckworth, *Grit: The Power of Passion and Perseverance* (Scribner, 2016), 143.
7. Gallup, *State of the American Workplace* (Gallup, 2017), prepared using Gallup's in-depth research and analytics.
8. Patrick L. Hill, Nicholas A. Turiano, David K. Mroczek, and Anthony L. Burrow, "Purpose in Life and All-Cause Mortality across Adulthood," *Psychological Science* 26, no. 10 (2015): 1482–86.
9. J. Martínez-Calderón, R. Santos-Rodríguez, and P. Barranco-Gallardo, "Meaning and Purpose in Life, Happiness, and Well-Being: A Systematic Review with Meta-Analysis," *Psycho-Oncology* 32, no. 5 (2023): 789–807.
10. Eric S. Kim, Shelley D. Hershner, and Victor J. Strecher, "Purpose in Life and Incidence of Sleep Disturbances among Older Adults," *Journal of Behavioral Medicine* 38, no. 3 (June 2015): 590–597, https://doi.org/10.1007/s10865-015-9635-4.
11. Anthony L. Burrow and R. Nathan Spreng, "Waiting with Purpose: A Reliable but Small Association between Purpose in Life and Impulsivity," *Personality and Individual Differences* 90 (2016): 187–189, https://doi.org/10.1016/j.paid.2015.11.010.
12. Ian D. Boreham, Nicola S. Schutte, "The Relationship between Purpose in Life and Depression and Anxiety: A Meta-Analysis," *Journal of Clinical Psychology* 79, no. 12 (December 2023): 2736–2767, https://doi.org/10.1002/jclp.23576.
13. Mount Sinai Medical Center, "Have a Sense of Purpose in Life? It May Protect Your Heart," ScienceDaily, March 6, 2015, accessed June 2, 2025, https://www.sciencedaily.com/releases/2015/03/150306132538.htm.
14. Boas Shamir and Galit Eilam, "'What's Your Story?' A Life-Stories Approach to Authentic Leadership Development," *The Leadership Quarterly* 16, no. 3 (2005): 395-417.

15. Anthony L. Burrow, "Beyond Finding Purpose: Motivating a Translational Science of Purpose Acquisition," *International Journal of Environmental Research and Public Health* 20, no. 12 (2023): 6091.
16. John C. Pingree Jr., "I Have a Work for Thee," *Ensign* or *Liahona*, Nov. 2017, 32.
17. Russell M. Nelson, *Accomplishing the Impossible: What God Does, What We Can Do* (Deseret Book, 2015), 147.
18. Stephen Jones, "Why LDS Young Men Leader Brad Wilcox Believes God's Grace Is The Key To Overcoming THIS New Epidemic," Nov. 26, 2023, by Let's Get Real with Stephen Jones, YouTube, https://youtu.be/mRfqe0Ig9YM?si=UK3NmRBMLgbov9Rh.
19. Dallin H. Oaks, "The Challenge to Become," *Ensign*, Nov. 2000, 32.
20. Dieter F. Uchtdorf, "It Works Wonderfully!," *Ensign* or *Liahona*, Nov. 2015, 23.
21. "You Were Born with Potential," Goodreads, accessed Aug. 1, 2025, https://www.goodreads.com/quotes/7337182-you-were-born-with-potential-you-were-born-with-goodness.
22. *Teachings of Presidents of the Church: David O. McKay* (2011), 22.
23. "The Purpose of Relief Society," *Ensign*, Jan. 2017, 7.
24. Bill George, Peter Sims, Andrew N. McLean, and Diana Mayer, "Discovering Your Authentic Leadership," *Harvard Business Review*, Feb. 2007, https://hbr.org/2007/02/discovering-your-authentic-leadership.
25. "The Past Is Never Dead," Goodreads, accessed Aug. 1, 2025, https://www.goodreads.com/quotes/12124-the-past-is-never-dead-it-s-not-even-past.
26. Viktor E. Frankl, *Man's Search for Meaning* (Beacon Press, 2006), 109.
27. William Damon, *The Path to Purpose: Helping Our Children Find Their Calling in Life* (Free Press, 2008), chap. 4.
28. Wong, P. T. P. (2019). The positive psychology of suffering and the deep-and-wide hypothesis. Frontiers in Psychology.
29. Neal A. Maxwell, remarks at Joseph S. Clark funeral, Feb. 23, 1996, quoted in in Bruce C. Hafen, *A Disciple's Life: The Biography of Neal A. Maxwell* (Deseret Book, 2002), 20.
30. Maxwell, N. A. (1990, April). Endure it well. General Conference of The Church of Jesus Christ of Latter-day Saints.
31. "Efforts and Courage," Goodreads, accessed Aug. 1, 2025, https://www.goodreads.com/quotes/1389030-efforts-and-courage-are-not-enough-without-purpose-and-direction.
32. "State of the Global Workplace: 2023 Report," Gallup, accessed Aug. 1, 2025, https://www.gallup.com/workplace/349484/state-of-the-global-workplace.aspx.
33. "2 Items President Uchtdorf Always Carries with Him—And You Should, Too," LDS Living, Dec. 16,. 2017, https://www.ldsliving.com/2-items-president-uchtdorf-always-carries-with-him-and-you-should-too/s/87289.
34. "Satan Trembles," BrainyQuote, accessed Aug. 1, 2025, https://www.brainyquote.com/quotes/william_cowper_156809.
35. Richard G. Scott, "First Things First," *Ensign*, May 2001, 7.

36. Marvin J. Ashton, "A Yearning for Home," *Ensign*, Nov. 1992, 23.
37. Tamara W. Runia, "Your Repentance Doesn't Burden Jesus Christ; It Brightens His Joy," *Liahona*, May 2025.
38. Jeffrey R. Holland, "An High Priest of Good Things to Come," *Ensign*, Nov. 1999, 38.
39. Sydney Smith, in *Wit and Wisdom of the Rev. Sydney Smith* (1856), 201.
40. Dieter F. Uchtdorf, "A Firmly Set Anchor," *Ensign*, Apr. 2014, 4.
41. Russell M. Nelson, "Revelation for the Church, Revelation for Our Lives," *Ensign* or *Liahona*, May 2018, 96.
42. José A. Teixeira, "Bonded to Jesus Christ: Becoming the Salt of the Earth," *Liahona*, Nov. 2024, 31.
43. "The Meaning of Life," Goodreads, accessed Aug. 1, 2025, https://www.goodreads.com/quotes/607827-the-meaning-of-life-is-to-find-your-gift-the.
44. Amy Wrzesniewski, "Crafting Your Job into a Calling," Feb. 28, 2022, *Yale Talk: Conversations with Peter Salovey* (podcast), https://salovey.yale.edu/writings-and-speeches/yale-talk/crafting-your-job-calling.
45. Uchtdorf, D. F. (2008, October). Lift where you stand. General Conference of The Church of Jesus Christ of Latter-day Saints.
46. James Clear, *Atomic Habits: An Easy & Proven Way to Build Good Habits & Break Bad Ones* (Avery, 2018), 38.
47. "Disappointment," Goodreads, accessed Aug. 1, 2025, https://www.goodreads.com/quotes/272015-disappointment-is-a-sort-of-bankruptcy---the-bankruptcy-of.
48. "What We Do Now," Goodreads, accessed Aug. 1, 2025, https://www.goodreads.com/quotes/366270-what-we-do-now-echoes-in-eternity.
49. D. Todd Christofferson, "Why the Church," *Ensign* or *Liahona*, Nov. 2015, 108.
50. Randall R. Ridd, "Living with Purpose: The Important of 'Real Intent'" (worldwide devotional for young adults, Jan. 11, 2015).
51. Ronald A. Rasband, "Increasing Talents to Build the Kingdom, Do the Lord's Work" (Brigham Young University–Idaho devotional, Jan. 2011), https://www.thechurchnews.com/2011/1/26/23227356/increasing-talents-to-build-the-kingdom-do-the-lords-work/.
52. Howard W. Hunter, "A More Excellent Way," *Ensign*, May 1992, 61.
53. Steven D. Shumway, "Participate to Prepare for Christ's Return," *Liahona*, May 2025.
54. Russell M. Nelson, "Your Savior and the Future Before You," *For the Strength of Youth*, Apr. 2023.
55. Ezra Taft Benson, "Jesus Christ—Gifts and Expectations" (Brigham Young University devotional, Dec. 10, 1974), 6, speeches.byu.edu.
56. "President Nelson Shares 3 Things Mormons Need to Accomplish the Impossible," LDS Living, Jan. 20, 2018, https://www.ldsliving.com/president-nelson-shares-3-things-mormons-need-to-accomplish-the-impossible/s/87516.

About the Author

Dustin Peterson has led high-impact leadership training and career coaching for more than fifteen years. He is the founder and CEO at Proof Leadership Group, a leadership consultancy focused on building outstanding cultures where people thrive. He has helped more than 250 companies and thousands of individuals do more of what they do best as a trainer, coach, and consultant in the private, public, and nonprofit sectors.

When not writing, training, or coaching, he enjoys training for triathlons, eating bacon, and cheering on Dallas sports teams.

Dustin completed his MS in educational leadership from Indiana University and his BS in communications at Brigham Young University–Idaho. He is the author of three other books and lives in Texas with his wife and four kids.

You can connect with Dustin at dustin@proofleadership.com, via Instagram @dustinpeterson, or by visiting his sites at www.proofleadership.com and www.dustinpeterson.org.

Scan to visit

https://dustinpeterson.org/